Praise for *The Reason*

"Fresh. Passionate. Powerful. Lacey Sturm does in *The Reason* what she has done her whole career—she tells the truth, sings the truth, dances the truth. Her story will blow you away, and her heart will touch you. Read *The Reason*. Just like her voice and presence, Lacey's writing compels and penetrates, and in the end she will change you."

Chap Clark, PhD, author of *Hurt 2.0:*
Inside the World of Today's Teenagers

"In a time where the gulf between sacred and secular seems to grow incrementally, Lacey bridges the gap with her soul-baring candor, raw passion, and prophetic insight. She communicates the comedy, tragedy, and triumph of her life story with fluidity and grace, and her message is timelessly impactful. It 'screams' of Jesus Christ, who is alive and active today, even in our darkest times, and the great news that no one is beyond his reach."

John L. Cooper, lead singer of Skillet

"At its core Lacey's story is one of hope. From desperation to redemption to victory, this is an amazing journey that, apart from God, would not be possible. Hers is a story that will encourage and challenge all who read it."

Michael W. Smith, singer and songwriter

"I have been fortunate to witness Lacey grow from singer/songwriter to wife to mommy to now author. She is an amazing soul with a heart like no other. Her life and her story have been such an encouragement to me, and I know this book will also inspire and change you forever."

Sonny Sandoval, lead singer of P.O.D.
and founding member of The Whosoevers

"Lacey has touched so many lives around the world through her music. Her story will hit your heart."

Ryan Ries, cofounder of The Whosoevers

"Lacey Sturm is a voice of hope to a hurting generation. In her book you will experience God's unstoppable heart for you and for those in your life who need a supernatural reset. Lacey's message is real, raw, and dripping with love. Dive in and be blessed!"

Nick Hall, founder and primary communicator of PULSE

THE
MYSTERY

FINDING TRUE LOVE
IN A WORLD OF BROKEN LOVERS

LACEY STURM

BakerBooks

a division of Baker Publishing Group
Grand Rapids, Michigan

Published by Baker Books
a division of Baker Publishing Group
P.O. Box 6287, Grand Rapids, MI 49516-6287
www.bakerbooks.com

Printed in the United States of America

Library of Congress Cataloging-in-Publication Data
Names: Sturm, Lacey, author.
Title: The mystery : finding true love in a world of broken lovers / Lacey Sturm.
Description: Grand Rapids : Revell, 2016. | Includes bibliographical references.
Identifiers: LCCN 2016020848 | ISBN 9780801016745 (pbk.)
Subjects: LCSH: Sturm, Lacey. | Rock musicians—United States—Biography. |
   Christian biography. | LCGFT: Biographies.
Classification: LCC ML420.S922 A3 2016 | DDC 277.3/083092 [B] —dc23
LC record available at https://lccn.loc.gov/2016020848

Main illustrations by Sherri DuPree-Bemis. Additional illustrations by Jordan Clarke.

Some details and names have been changed for privacy purposes.

Published in association with Yates & Yates, www.yates2.com.

16 17 18 19 20 21 22   7 6 5 4 3 2 1

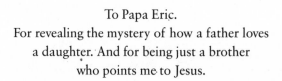

To Papa Eric.
For revealing the mystery of how a father loves
a daughter. And for being just a brother
who points me to Jesus.

Contents

Contents

PART 1

A WORLD OF BROKEN LOVERS

Love ceases to be a demon only when he ceases to be a god. . . . God is love, but love is not God. . . . The rebellious slogan "All for Love" is really love's death warrant (date of execution, for the moment, left blank).

C. S. Lewis[1]

1

THE MYSTERY OF
Being Royal

An Introduction

> You thought you were being made into a decent little
> cottage, but [God] is building a palace. He intends to
> come and live in it Himself.
>
> C. S. Lewis[1]

*S*he always smelled like cocoa butter and summertime. My
mother's arms were smooth and soft. I watched her jack up
our car to change a flat tire countless times. Every time I saw her
do this, I knew she could easily hold that car up on her own if she
wanted to. Her strength was something supernatural, despite her
petite frame. Her wrists, delicate. Her hands, graceful. Yes, her
fingertips were calloused from playing her guitar, but this was the
only hint of roughness on her body.

Her arms carried me. And along with my grandmother's and aunt's, they were the only arms I ever remembered carrying me.

A woman's embrace was all I ever knew for the first few years of my life.

One Halloween our family was walking in a neighborhood at dusk. Below the fluffy ballerina tutu, my short three-year-old legs hurried to keep up with the excitement of the miniature pirate I was following. I took three times the steps my older brother took on our long walk. My legs tired, so I asked my mom to hold me, over and over.

Up: walk. Down: trick-or-treat. Up: walk. Down: trick-or-treat. Finally, my mother wearied.

"Just walk. Stop complaining. I'm tired too."

That's when I felt his hands. They were large and warm under my arms. They wrapped all the way around me—from my sternum to my spine. Gentle. Safe. Strong. He lifted me higher than I'd ever been lifted before. He handled me like I was fine china.

He set me in the curve of his firm arm—I fit perfectly. His rough skin was covered by the thick, tangled hair on his forearms. He smelled like a Christmas tree and a wood fire. I don't remember his face. Only the deep lines around his mouth as he smiled down at me.

I remember his joy when he held me—like it was a privilege. This is my first memory of a man's embrace. I blushed all over. My little, tense body relaxed in his cuddle. I don't remember falling asleep, but I know it happened quickly.

I never knew his name. He was only a friend of a friend of our family. My mother doesn't even

remember him. But I remember his embrace. Afterward, I had a quiet aching to experience that sense of safe, masculine purity again.

The Reality of Absence

My father missed the opportunity to love me in person. I never met him. He was in prison for a while. I remember him sending me a Christmas present one year. I wasn't resentful that he wasn't there. In fact, I would've told you I didn't need a dad. But his absence was significant. I didn't realize the effect as a young girl, but it turns out, it did matter.

I figured I could make up my own reality, though. I envisioned myself as independent. *I'm not fatherless—don't treat me differently.* I defended myself. *I* had to do what my dad would do. But false realities bring pain. I always felt like a burden. Like I was a weight on others and society—one they wanted to ignore.

I was fatherless. And that seemingly small part of my identity, in many ways, molded an orphan heart in me.

When I encountered love my orphan heart rejected it because it felt like the smartest thing to do. My philosophy was *They will reject me, so I will reject them first. They don't get to hurt me.*

I did this often. I intended never to owe anyone a kindness I couldn't pay back. I stayed "out of the way." I did my best not to cost anyone anything.

I was suspicious of gifts. *What do they want? What are they trying to pull? How are they trying to trap me?* I thought. I couldn't imagine I was worth anyone's time, money, pain, or inconvenience. I didn't see myself as a blessing, so how could I trust in unconditional love? When you see yourself as a burden, nothing is free—especially love.

But that's not reality. It may seem like it, but that is a lie from hell. I've learned another way to view myself. It's the way God intends each person on earth to view themselves. God offers us another reality: *his*.

The Reality of the Kingdom

I was born a temple.

A living, breathing temple.

My Creator dreamed of me. Not my mother, who did not plan me. Not my father, who was not expecting a second child. In my mother's womb, with sacred materials, the King of heaven and earth knit together a temple. He protected me so that I would grow.

By the time I was sixteen, I found myself restless and empty, feeling defiled with no way to be fixed. I was ready to die for lack of purpose. I *wanted* to die because I couldn't see that anyone wanted me to live. I didn't know there was a God who had created me with a purpose in mind. I didn't know I was a temple. I didn't know that after I sold myself to death, I had been bought back by the King of heaven, who is life.

He knew I'd sense something was missing. He knew I'd search. He knew I'd blaspheme. He knew I'd hate. He knew I'd choose death and adopt an orphan heart.

But.

As I heard Jon Foreman once say, "There is a song, and it is uniquely yours! It reverberates in your heart."

Once I understood the song of my heart I realized the truth for the first time. My King stood at the door to my soul, knocking in time with my heart song. He dreamed of me and rescued me. Then he drew up heavenly papers and sealed them with his blood and adopted me—his daughter.

From orphan to princess in a heartbeat. I was born into the mystery of his love.

The world labeled me a bastard from conception.

An accident.

A mistake.

A parasitical-type creature who burdens society.

An unworthy cost.

Another statistic who causes the legitimate citizens of good society to groan, roll their eyes, and sigh, "Do we really have to put up with this?"

My mother knew what it was like to feel unwanted, and she refused to let them talk her into labeling me that way.

"People may make mistakes, but it's God who makes babies," she'd say through a tightly set jaw. "There is no such thing as an illegitimate child."

My mother watched miracles of provision break past all odds from one moment to the next. So she believed in those miracles for my life as well. As she looked for the miracles, waiting on them to come, she always found them.

If God wanted to end my life, then he could have taken it himself in those seven months of my mother's pregnancy, or those twelve years of my childhood, or my seven teenage years.

But instead of taking my life, God protected it.

Over and over, as I moved from situation to situation like a gypsy across the southeast United States, God protected, corrected, and provided.

Why?

Because he is my heavenly Father.

Because I wasn't born a bastard. None of us are.

My Orphan Lifestyle

Still, so many of us choose an orphan lifestyle, like I did for most of my life. I wrestled with being fatherless. Finally, I dismissed the idea of needing a father and embraced an orphan identity. I found a cold kind of peace in deciding I wouldn't expect anyone to help me. I would protect myself, provide for myself, and decide for myself what was right and wrong. But all the boundaries I made were dotted lines, always shifting and changing with the wind. As an orphan I not only had to be God for myself but I also felt the need to be God for every other orphan I came across. When I failed myself and others one too many times, I wanted to die.

When you think of yourself as God, you can condemn yourself and others in the most hellish ways. When you have God as your father, you can rest in his goodness, sovereignty, and justice. But if there is no God, *you* must be the judge.

But in the Gospel of Luke, Jesus said:

> Do not judge, and you will not be judged. Do not condemn, and you will not be condemned. Forgive, and you will be forgiven. Give, and it will be given to you. A good measure, pressed down, shaken together and running over, will be poured into your lap. For with the measure you use, it will be measured to you. . . . Can the blind lead the blind? Will they not both fall into a pit? (Luke 6:37–39)

Whenever I wanted to see someone beaten for being a liar, I would suddenly see a liar in myself. Indeed, our judgment of others comes back to us but even worse, as Jesus said, "pressed down, shaken together and running over." I condemned liars as deserving a beating, but I condemned my own lying self as deserving of death. The truth was I hated the way leaders hurt the people they were leading, and then found myself trying to be a good god for others only to fall into a pit with them falling with me. I hated myself for not being good enough—and for not being god enough.

The truth is no one is god enough to be God except God himself. We are reflections of him in so many ways. But we are only the creatures. We are not the Creator. Apart from knowing our heavenly Father and all that he made us for, we will always come up short of what we are meant to be and experience as his creation.

We are made to be children of the King of heaven.

We Are Royal Superheroes

You and I are made to be royalty.

Each one of us shines a unique facet of God's light and love into the world. God gave us unique DNA, fingerprints, voices, and perspectives. We are living colors on God's palette. And this life he's painting is made more beautiful, more distinct, richer, and deeper when we embrace the fullness God intends for us—not when we try to be someone else or compare and condemn one another or ourselves. In the refuge of our heavenly identity we blaze. And eventually that light spills into the world—the blazing rainbow of God's intended purpose. And as we honor our uniqueness and the uniqueness of those around us, we will see miraculous glory and encounter the fullness of God's beauty.

God made us to be spiritual warrior royalty who spiritually war for the truth in a world of lies. God made us superheroes, living supernatural lives of love that bring healing.

We're to live as citizens of heaven, on earth.

We're meant to stand up in our purposes.

We're meant to fight lies by choosing to believe the truth about who we are, about who God is, and about who others are. This breaks the chains that hold humanity back from our destiny of love, peace, unity, grace, and joy.

When I was a passionate, proud, angry, hate-filled young atheist, most of the time I was deeply depressed and cynical. Every day, I struggled with self-loathing. God was always waiting for me to hear his dream for my life.

Lacey, you are my beloved princess. If only you will be my daughter, then I will be your Father. This is what my beloved King of heaven longed to speak to my orphan heart. But I couldn't understand this.

When I was a child, questions hung in the air above my restless heart that knew nothing of what it meant to have a father. *What does* father *mean? And what does that have to do with me?*

So Mysterious

A father provides identity. Without a father to tell me who I was, I let the world tell me. But I was being lied to. And in silent moments, uncertainty threatened to suffocate me. Once I encountered my heavenly Father's loving gaze, I felt known beyond what I even knew of myself. And here's the beautiful part of it all: when I began to live in my *knownness*, the words, intentions, and perceptions of the world didn't matter. And I no longer care what the world might try to call me when I *know* who I am. And that confidence creates a certain hiddenness—a *mystery*. When a person can reject the world's perception of them, the world says, "Wait—well then, who are you?"

Suddenly they become alluring.

I want to take you on the journey of how I discovered the mystery of my heavenly Father and how that discovery clothed me in mystery too. I want to recount how I struggled through an affair—one that almost took my life. And so I need to walk you through my early life as a Christian. It was a time when I questioned my faith in God and had to choose whether I was going to *really* believe in him or not. What I discovered changed my life.

True love is freedom. True love is risk. True love is faith and trust. True love is beautiful, passionate, pure, and safe. True love is life itself. True love has no rival.

2

THE MYSTERY OF
Needing to Be Needed

Cursed is the one who trusts in man, who draws strength from mere flesh.

Jeremiah the prophet[1]

*T*he enemy of your soul will always send along someone inappropriate to meet a need that is unmet in you.

Before I became a Christian I would just go up to a guy and kiss him, thinking I was "empowering" him. But after becoming a Christian I found sexuality to be much more sacred than I had viewed it before. I accepted that sexuality was meant to have boundaries that made it glow with a precious, committed exclusivity. I didn't understand that truth. As a Christian I was learning to safeguard my body, but I didn't yet realize I also had to safeguard my soul. I didn't understand that in the same way that kissing a guy would open him up to further romance I might not have intended, so my "kissing" someone's soul could do that too.

The result of my naïveté manifested itself in a relationship that taught me the destructive nature of believing the lie that we can't control who we fall in love with. I didn't realize the importance of being purposeful with my heart, emotions, and displays of love. If we are not purposeful we risk painfully falling in and out of love, over and over, according to our circumstances, whims, and ignorance.

My Teenage Marriage

The day after my divorce was finalized, there were strange waves of both relief and mourning rolling over me while I tied on my apron and stared blankly at the schedule sheet hanging on the wall. Aaron says that when he asked me to marry him, we were both too young. I was nineteen but I didn't feel young. I didn't feel naïve when I told God and Aaron all that "till death do us part" stuff on our wedding day. I didn't feel young when I said it at all. I felt mature and committed.

But two years later I felt like I was emotionally reliving junior high school. My heart felt like it was ripped down the same old scar from then. Maybe I was too young to give my heart away in junior high. Maybe I was too young to give my heart away at nineteen. Maybe Aaron was right. But maybe it didn't have to do with my age at all. Maybe it had to do with giving my heart away.

The smell of a Texas winter morning mixed with Schoepf's barbecue smoke filled the back room by my boss's office. She had scheduled us on opposite days like Aaron and I asked her to. He had gotten me a job making extra money at the barbeque place where he worked. They always needed extra help. His band was traveling more now, so he wasn't working much anyway.

Things had fallen apart between us.

Aaron had already romantically familiarized himself with a very pretty and less complicated female. I had already found solace in a male friend, Nathan, whom I was growing increasingly close to at work. He appreciated the nuances of my heart that Aaron never noticed. After three months of uncertainty, tears, and chaos, I was officially a twenty-one-year-old divorcee.

Two Lonely Married People See Each Other

Nathan was only a friend, but I never wanted to leave when we were together. I never wanted to hang up when we talked. My heart burned when his name came up on my phone. I ignored all of these feelings because he was married, and up until now so was I. It only made sense that I would be thinking of him the day after I signed my divorce papers.

No matter how close we seemed to get emotionally, and how I may have questioned if it was right, I was not willing to let our "friendship" go. It met too many unmet needs in my heart. It nursed too many wounds. It brought me to "life" in ways I had always felt dead. And most of all, Nathan made me feel needed. He made me feel like I could save him when no one else could. This is how my orphan heart came to life. When I could think of myself as a savior.

I didn't realize that not only could I not save Nathan but trying to would destroy us both. Still, the chemical reaction in my heart of feeling needed was something I had been missing. I remember the night when that deep connection first occurred.

It was on the first night we were both scheduled to close. He was older, and funny, but I didn't notice anything beyond that. There was a small birthday celebration going on between the employees and someone was passing out beer to everyone. There was a lot of laughter and joking and camaraderie.

"I don't drink," I answered when they offered me one. "But tell Drew I said happy birthday anyway."

"Yeah, right, the prude Christian girl. You need a drink more than any of us!"

They rolled their eyes.

"You don't know what I need," I yelled as I took the leftover jalapeno cornbread to the back so I could pack it up and take it home with me. I almost hit Nathan as I swung the door open and someone yelled out, "Nathan, did you get one of these?" holding up a beer.

"Naw, man, you know I'm sober! Two years and fourteen days."

"Come on, Nathan, you're not gonna celebrate your boy Drew's birthday? How can you be so selfish?" they chided. Everyone was joining in now.

I was appalled.

These grown people were acting so childish. Everyone knew that Nathan was a recovering alcoholic. Didn't they know, or at least hear stories of, what it was like to get sober? That it was hard enough without some junior high–style peer pressure?

The loudest one, who was supposedly a Christian, was always making fun of Christians who didn't drink, talking about Jesus like the great liberator of religious sobriety, turning water into gallons of wine. But didn't Jesus also sympathize with our weaknesses? Couldn't they have a little sympathy and shut up?

Nathan just laughed and joined in, making fun of himself along with them. But when he turned his face away, I could tell he was trying not to show his sadness. When I saw that look on his face, I felt my heart twist with compassion. He seemed deeply alone. It made me so angry at the others who couldn't understand.

I understood what it was like to have a loved one struggle with alcoholism, so I wanted to encourage Nathan in his desire to stay sober. I could still remember my stepdad Michael's struggle with addiction and alcoholism from my childhood. I remember being seven years old and seeing the half-empty beer bottle fly past my mother, barely missing her wincing face and shattering against the house.

"Get in the house now!" she had screamed at me.

I had been so scared to leave her. Was he going to kick the door in again? Were the police coming again? I cried and obeyed. I looked down at my two-year-old little sister. Fear had drained all the color from her face. I dragged her to our bedroom and closed the door. "Everything is going to be okay. Mom is taking care of it. Don't worry," I said. She cried, sucked her thumb, and twisted her hair.

Wasn't that man screaming at my mother and throwing things at her the same soft-spoken man who used to rock me to sleep? Michael wasn't mean like this. Wasn't he the closest thing to a daddy I had? And now, after this fight, I just knew. I knew it was over. I knew he was leaving. That was the last I saw of him until years later, after he had finished rehab. He went back and forth, doing well and then struggling to stay clean.

When I saw Nathan trying to be strong, I wanted to make sure he knew someone appreciated his lonely sobriety and celebrated him for making a healthy choice that night.

My Savior Complex

After everyone else had gone, Nathan and I closed up in silence. I could tell he was absorbed in thought. He stood at the door, holding it open, waiting while I put my apron away and clocked out. He smiled when I thanked him and walked through. His smile seemed customary, forced. So I asked him, my heart still wrenching.

"Are you okay?"

Still wearing his business hat and fake smile, he answered. "Yeah, I'm fine. Just got to get home to the kiddos."

"But it just seems like you work so much. Like the only people you really get to be around is all of us here. And it doesn't seem like anyone gets what you've been through."

His smile melted away slowly. His eyes grew wider.

Tears filled his eyes before he looked away quickly, holding his head up so they wouldn't fall.

He gave a nervous chuckle. Then he looked back at me, the dimness of the street light that was gathering moths and mosquitos changing the shadows on his face. He seemed more composed now, as if he was trying to put on his business hat that had gotten knocked off by my words.

"It just seems lonely," I mumbled, looking at the ground.

He was quiet. I finally looked back up, and his eyes were wide and wondering, searching me deeply. No business smile could mask his sadness and, for the first time since I had met him, he didn't try to hide it.

"I've always felt the same way about you. You always seem lonely too," he said.

My heart dropped to the bottom of my feet. I didn't expect him to respond that way. I just wanted him to know that he shouldn't give up trying to stay sober. I didn't think he ever noticed me. And now that he said it, he made me face something I never would admit.

I was married.

And someone was finally calling me out: I had never felt so lonely in my life. Nathan and I grew closer. Aaron and I grew apart. I thought through these memories as I stared at that schedule sheet hanging on the wall, wondering about my future.

The enemy of our souls will always send someone inappropriate to meet an unmet need in our life. What was this unmet need inside of me that moved me toward Nathan? Was I just plain old naïve, or was there something rooted much deeper that pushed me into this?

Nathan did not need me to help him through his tough struggle with staying sober, but because of my orphan mentality I felt like he did. I didn't realize there were better options out there for him to get help. I didn't realize that I didn't need Nathan to help me either.

This was a trick from the enemy to make us both feel like the saviors neither one of us could really be for one another. We needed community and friendship. Finding it in each other in a vacuum was only a dangerous path to destroying our hearts. What seemed so perfectly fit together would fall apart one day soon. What felt like the answer to everything in each other would soon be the death of everything in the future.

What I needed most was someone *I could trust* to tell me that I should run from this situation. God provided loving voices along the way to warn me that "the bridge was out" on the road I was traveling with Nathan. But because I had an orphan mindset, I didn't know how to trust. I only knew how to be suspicious of father figures. So when a loving father figure came to warn me, I didn't recognize him. I was more comfortable with the orphanness in Nathan that was leading me toward death than I was with the healthy fatherly love from a man I knew that was calling me to safety, health, and life.

Erica Gascon

Meet Erica Gascon. She is a hero to me because her story is like mine but is also very different. I love the way we went through similar situations but because of our differences we shine with a unique glory through them. She is eloquent and thoughtful—a wonderful learner and teacher.

Here is a note to you from Erica.

Dear Reader,

We are called to live in the present, learn from the past, hope for the future, and focus on eternity. Instead we live in the past, distract ourselves from the present, attempt to dictate the future, and neglect eternity. It is no wonder that so many of us often feel so lost. We spend our days living in direct contradiction to how our Creator designed us to live.

If I could, I would go back to my twelve-year-old self and say, "Each day you have a choice to take a path; one of lightness or one of darkness. Choose wisely! With each step down the dark road, the light path will dim. It will gradually become harder to see, and one day you may find yourself in utter darkness. Each day you choose to walk in the sunshine will be one of true maturity. It will not always be easy, and you won't always be able to see the next step. But there is a peace that resides on this path, a true peace that can never be felt when walking in the dark."

Love,

Erica Gascon
wife, mother, writer

3

THE MYSTERY OF
an Orphan Identity

I will not leave you as orphans; I will come to you.

Jesus of Nazareth[1]

*Y*ou don't really believe in all that fairy-tale BS, right?"

He was the lead singer of the headlining band. We were the new, little, and local opening band. We stood in a group outside our van, chatting.

"You guys need to have some fun and quit worrying about some imaginary God striking you with lightning! You need to live!" He inhaled deeply on his joint, raised his eyebrows like we were missing out, and walked away.

That scene floated in my head later that night as I lay in my bed, thinking. Were we always going to be playing the local bar scene with bands who could care less about our souls? I wondered how we would be able to keep up with our faith, going into such crazy places.

Our guitarist, Jared, was only fifteen years old. I thought about some of our recent shows: the sexual advances, the offers for drugs and parties, the hostility and mocking about us being Christians.

I realized we needed some kind of band pastor. But I had never heard of such a thing. Where do you find a band pastor? I was about to drift off to sleep when the name *Eric Patrick* scrolled across my brain.

Who Is Eric Patrick?

From the time I was ten until I was sixteen years old, I was an out-spoken atheist who hated Christians. In my first book, *The Reason*, I talked about this time in my life and how God rescued me from suicide at age sixteen through a miraculous series of events. Not long after that encounter I had with God, one of the Christians I used to make fun of at school found out about my change of heart.

Scott was the one cool Christian in junior high. He loved punk rock, skateboarding, and multicolored facial hair. As a fourteen-year-old, know-it-all, loud-mouthed atheist, the only reason I didn't write Scott off completely, like I did every other Christian, was because he didn't back down when I questioned his strange, persistent love for Jesus. He wasn't afraid of all of us making fun of his faith and his sobriety. He almost seemed to enjoy it sometimes. He did his fair share of making logical fun of our drunkenness and stupidity as well. So we respected him for that.

When I returned to Texas from Mississippi as a Christian, Scott showed up at my mom's house unannounced. I opened the door to his familiar green hair and broad, crooked smirk.

"So I hear you love Jesus now," he boasted like he had won a bet. Not even a hello.

I cracked up.

"Okay, okay, you won. I'm one of you weirdos now," I answered.

"So, do you wanna go to church with me, then?" he pressed.

My heart leapt.

I hadn't been to church since I came to visit my mom for the summer.

We jumped in his orange VW beetle and drove into a ghetto neighborhood within Arlington, Texas. The sign in front of the building read "Door of Hope Church." The sign looked lame. So did the church, honestly. It looked like some place you'd worry about the fray on the bottom of your jeans being offensive and hope your shoes didn't squeak. I looked at my green-haired friend and relaxed a little, realizing if they were going to judge me here, at least they were going to judge Scotty too. We walked down a little hallway and turned into a tiny room where there were two other people about our age talking in a circle with a slightly older guy, who was wearing an acoustic guitar and had long brown hair parted down the middle and tucked behind his ears. His jeans were baggy and frayed at the bottom like mine. His Doc Martin boots looked fitting for a grungy college kid.

"This is Eric," said Scotty. "He's the youth pastor."

Eric the Youth Pastor

I was surprised to hear his position in such a stuffy building and wondered about how people got to become youth pastors. I said hello, and since there were no chairs I sat on the floor. I thought we must be early because no one else was there. Two more boys straggled in. They looked about twelve years old.

"All right," Eric said. "We're gonna go ahead and worship."

This is it? I thought to myself. I had never seen such a small group of people assemble in a church for "worship." There was a grand total of seven people in the room. Scott, Eric, me, the two other people about my age, and the two twelve-year-olds. I would have guessed that if only six people show up for church, someone would cancel. But the four older people closed their eyes to worship, while the two twelve-year-old boys simultaneously began to pick their noses. So I closed my eyes too.

Less than one minute into the song, I felt like heaven opened and I was in front of God himself. Peace filled the room and began to speak to my heavy heart about all the stress I was carrying. Peace wrapped around my mind as I sang. I could feel peace about all the problems going on in my house, as if all my problems were known and cared about in heaven. I sensed there was a grand purpose for all my struggles that would unfold in the perfect time. My soul was drinking deeply. I was healing inside.

This profound moment was occurring within me and the only music was coming from Eric on his acoustic guitar, Scotty on his beat up Fender jazz bass (plugged into a cheap Crate amp), and our voices. It wasn't excellent music, but it was coming from hearts that were used to worshiping God no matter the circumstances. I believe it was those few hearts of worship that opened heaven.

I opened my eyes as they ended the music, and the two twelve-year-old boys were now pinching each other, trying to see who could suffer the most pain in the most silent way possible. I pulled my knees up to my chest and wrapped my arms around them, feeling safe and open-hearted as Eric began to speak.

He talked about heaven, hell, revival, and the brokenness of Arlington, Texas. He showed us a video of what happened in other parts of the world when people worshiped and prayed. The Spirit of God would move in these places, and all kinds of miracles happened.

He quoted 2 Chronicles 7:14 in a loud, desperate voice. "If my people, who are called by my name, will humble themselves and pray and seek my face and turn from their wicked ways, then I will hear from heaven, and I will forgive their sin and will heal their land."

I was so moved with faith by all I heard that I wanted to weep. I wanted to worship and pray and never stop until God healed the brokenness in our city. And I never missed an opportunity to hear Eric speak or lead worship after that.

Reconnecting with Eric

I started to argue with God about the unreasonable suggestion that I would somehow be able to reconnect with Eric and that he would agree to be our band pastor.

"But he's married, and has at least one child that I know of, and how could we ever afford to pay him enough to provide for his family, to take time to pastor us like we would need? I don't know where he lives, what he's doing, or anything about him at all anymore."

But the image of Eric and his wife, Sarah, persisted in my head. I was so exhausted and wanted my brain to shut off, but I couldn't make it stop. Finally, I spoke out loud to God: "How would I even get their number?"

Call information, came the thought.

"But Eric Patrick is such a common name. There's probably a million of them. And I don't even know if he is in Arlington anymore," I protested out loud in my empty room.

The urge to call information became so invasive that I begrudgingly got out of my bed and, with sheer annoyed obedience coupled with very little faith, dialed information.

"Are there any Eric Patricks in Arlington, Texas?"

"Hold on, please." Pause. "No Eric Patrick in Arlington."

I was relieved to finally get a *no* so I could give up and go to sleep. But I was also surprised. I figured I'd at least have to call a dozen Eric Patricks to even begin looking for him.

"Thank you."

I was about to hang up when I heard the phrase—*DFW*—almost audibly in my head. I barely got it out of my mouth in time.

"Um, can you check DFW, please?"

The operator spoke quickly, sounding annoyed.

"Hold again, please."

I waited.

"I have one E. Patrick, in DeSoto."

"Can I have that number, please?"

Click. I thought she'd hung up on me, but then the numbers came in an electronic voice. I wrote them down and dialed, still with almost zero faith but hoping I could sleep after trying. A woman answered the phone.

"Hello?" I didn't think about what I was going to say so I stumbled through my introduction. "Is this Eric Patrick's residence?"

"Yes?" came the cautious reply.

"The same Eric Patrick who used to be a youth pastor at Door of Hope Church in Arlington, Texas?"

"Yes?"

"My name is Lacey. I used to be in that youth group. I've started a band and I looked up your number so I could ask if Eric might be at all interested in being our band pastor?"

Silence.

"Oh! Hi, Lacey. Of course, I remember you. Let me go get Eric," she said.

I waited, feeling really stupid. The request sounded so ridiculous. I could hear kids playing in the background, and knew that this was probably a psychotic proposal to offer a family I didn't even know anymore. After a brief moment Eric got on the line.

"Hello? Lacey! How are you? Hey, we are going to be praying about what you asked. Maybe we should meet?"

Confronting My Orphan Identity

A couple weeks later Eric arranged a retreat for the band and we all met at Sarah's parents' place in the country. For a week we rehearsed every day in this awesome, mildew-scented shed full of spider webs. We also read a book by Watchman Nee as a group. We talked about our history and spiritual lives.

One afternoon we gathered in the living room of a spare trailer on their property. Eric sat on the floor in the corner, looking at all of us. He said, "I've been praying for you guys all week—praying that God would show me how to encourage you."

He paused for a moment. I could tell he was wondering if he should explain more before he shared what was on his heart. Finally, he just said it.

"I feel like the Lord wants to remove your orphan identity."

Immediately I saw the image of a dolphin in my head. I had so little connection with the word *orphan* that when I heard it, I related it to a dolphin just because the words sounded similar.

I had no idea what Eric was saying. He explained the role of a father.

"Fathers protect, provide, and correct," he said.

Unknowingly, I carried an immense amount of baggage related to fathers. This heavy weight distorted my perspective of men and the role of fathers in general.

Protect, *provide*, and *correct* sounded like things police officers do. I couldn't imagine what it would look like for a father to protect me. Growing up, I'd learned that expecting a father to protect you was like sitting on a broken chair. It might look like having a father was protective, but that was, in my experience, a sad illusion.

Hero Note:
Evan Tachoir

Meet Evan Tachoir. He is a hero to me because
after all he has seen in his life he continues
to pursue the heart of his heavenly Father. He
could have easily become bitter and found reasons to write off faith and God. But instead of writing off God in the face of his pain, Evan embraced him.
Because of that, he is able to be creative in unique ways and display how
glory comes out of darkness if we let it.

Here's a note to you, from Evan.

Dear Reader,

God is better than you think. If I could go back and
give my teenage self advice, I'd say, "There's hope beyond
the hurt you feel from your mother's suicide and from
being picked on in school. Keep holding on. It will be a
lonely few years, but there is payoff in the future. Let
go of wanting acceptance from people at school; you
are not defined by what they think and say. It's what
your heavenly Father thinks of you that defines you. He
loves you, despite all your shortcomings. His patience
will stick with you, even when you don't stick with him.
He is a creative, unique God who created a creative and
unique you. He loves you just the way he made you. He
loves you so you can love yourself. Once you can do this,

you can love others and be free to be the dreamer you're created to be."

with the Father's love,
Evan (3PFD)
husband, rap artist

Cause life wasn't always great. I went through some desperate times. Lost my mom at thirteen. I stayed in my bed cryin'. Nothing in my head straight. No way that I could rest, even set a death date, to follow in her footsteps. April 15, '99, said I wanna take my life. Wrapped in pain and strife, until I was saved by Jesus Christ. Though I was abandoned here, he came and paid my ransom here. It's 2009, ten years later. I'm still standing here.

3PFD, "Evan's Song"

All of these questions were rooted in this one:
Do I have a Heavenly Father or am I an orphan?

4

THE MYSTERY OF
Fatherlessness

If it were classified as a disease, fatherlessness would be an epidemic worthy of attention as a national emergency. . . . Fatherlessness is associated with almost every societal ill facing our country's children.

National Center for Fathering[1]

You don't need to try to punish your dad yourself. Pray that the eyes of his heart would be willing to turn to your heavenly Father in brokenness. He too can experience transformation.

Tamy Elam

*F*athers *protect?*

When I was in second grade, there was a girl my age named Anna living in our apartment complex who asked me to come over. She lived with her father. He was a single dad. Anna didn't remember her mother, who'd left them when Anna was a baby. She showed me her Barbie dolls and we played together in her room for a while before her dad came in.

"I'm going to work, but Jonathan will be here, so if you need anything ask him."

"No!" My friend cried and begged her daddy to stay. I was surprised by her hysterics. She was too old to be crying the way she was. Her brother, who was a couple years older, walked by and saw her clinging to their daddy's leg and mercilessly mocked her.

"'Wah, wah, wah, I want my daddy!' You're pathetic, you little baby! You annoy everyone with your whining. He's not going to stay here. No one wants to stay here with you crying like a baby!"

"Shut up!" she yelled through her tears.

Her father scolded her harshly. "You are not a baby, so stop acting like one. I have to go to work like I do every day and your brother is right. Your whining is not going to make me stay. Now let go of my leg or you're going to get it. That's enough!"

She let go and slumped down into a ball on the floor, covering her face to smother her sobs.

"I love you," he said firmly. "That's why I have to go to work. So I can feed you and pay our bills. I'll see you tonight."

She wouldn't raise her face, so he kissed her on the top of her head and left her on the floor. I handed her a Barbie and tried to comfort her, "We can still play though," I said. She took it but stayed curled up in her little ball. When we heard the front door shut, she sat up and said to me with big, urgent eyes, "Is your momma home? Can we go to your house? Please?"

"No, my momma isn't home. It's only my little brother's daddy. But you can come over still if you want."

"I don't want to go over where your brother's daddy is! Only if your mom is there." She was whispering now.

"What's wrong?" I asked her.

"It's Jonathan. He's my cousin. He's a teenager. When my daddy leaves, he makes me sit on his lap under the covers and he hurts me really bad."

I was scared for her.

"Anna, why don't you tell your daddy? He could stop him." I thought about her daddy and how big and strong he was, and how skinny and weak her cousin looked.

"Because Jonathan says that if I tell my daddy then my daddy will kill him. Then my daddy will go to jail and I will never see my daddy again. And since I don't have a momma, I will go to a place where kids go that don't have parents. And he said that they will hurt me even worse in that place than he does."

Just as she finished saying those words Jonathan's voice rang out from the living room. "Anna? Come here, Anna."

I felt a wave of fear rush over me.

I whispered to her, "You have to tell your daddy, Anna! Come with me to my house."

"No! I can't! And you have to promise me never to tell anyone or I will never see my daddy again!"

"Anna?" Jonathan's voice was getting louder and sounded annoyed.

"I have to go now."

She put down her Barbie and walked slowly into the living room. I watched her stand by the chair where he was sitting as he leaned over and whispered into her ear. She hung her head and walked quickly back to the room where I was waiting for her.

"He wants you to come and sit with him," she said with searching eyes. I could tell she was almost begging me to obey quickly, and almost hopeful that he would leave her alone if I went.

"I'm gonna leave. Come with me! Please!" I begged her.

"No, please don't leave!" she pleaded.

I was looking past her as she pleaded with me. My eyes were locked on the front door just past Jonathan's chair. His back was facing the door while he watched television. She was standing in front of me when I bolted, so I had to push her. I sprinted to the door, slung it open, and ran the fastest I'd ever run in my life. I ran all the way home.

These Kinds of Men

Since I can remember, my mom had warned me about these kinds of men. I knew to watch out for that kind of thing. Because of my mom, I knew what to do in that moment and I am thankful. My heart still grieves over Anna. I kept my childish promise to never tell anyone and I've always regretted that mistake. I should have told someone. I hated myself when I was older every time I thought of how I'd done the wrong thing in not telling someone.

I realize now that when I was a child I thought most men would do bad things to children and women and each other if you left them alone. Sexual abuse was almost always assumed. It is a sad and destructive thing to judge all men in such a terrible way, but that is the way I saw the world for most of my life.

My experience taught me that fathers, or men in general, do not protect us. Quite the opposite.

I thought that maybe a good woman could change a man. Isn't that what I learned from the media? It was the woman who saved the man in my generation, not the other way around. Yeah, I saw those moments in old movies, where the prince would save the princess, but I never took that seriously. I viewed only women as being the ones who were safe, moral, wise, and loving. I saw men, on the other hand, as foolish, scary, selfish, and always looking for ways to get away with doing hurtful things. I thought this was the way fathers always treated their families.

But thank God this isn't true. I see that now, but I couldn't see it then.

If I saw a man being affectionate toward his daughter, I related it to a danger sign. I assumed that this affection was sexual in nature and just a front to get what he really wanted. I debased and animalized men with my prejudice, thinking they were all perverse in nature.

This is the most destructive thing to think about sincere love. If you and I believe sincere love is rooted in perversion, we will never see love's purity and goodness. Our beliefs are powerful. We can destroy pure love by our unbelief in it, and we can project unhealthy love into something healthy just by suspecting the worst. In the right context, suspicion can be true discernment and wisdom to protect ourselves and our loved ones, but in the wrong context it can sabotage otherwise beautiful and healing relationships. We must always examine our souls and pray to be rid of any destructive prejudice. We must also remember that God has made a way for all evil to be transformed into glory, healing, and deliverance, no matter what side of the evil we are on.

Fathers Steal and Use the Rent Money on Drugs

Father's *provide*? I wondered what Eric meant by that. *What? What do fathers provide?*

I remember staying with my best friend Adrianne for a couple weeks during one summer. I adored her parents. They'd been married for years. Her father kept a steady job, and he'd bring everyone their favorite treats home from the store after work. He and his wife were always joking, giggling, or laughing hysterically. They seemed to be the best of friends. That's why I didn't understand what we were doing sitting in the dark, all piled in the car, waiting for him outside a shady motel room.

People entered then exited. Every time someone entered and left, I noticed my friend's mom crying. She was quiet, but her tears kept falling. She was trying to figure out what to do, but I didn't understand. Finally, she turned to me and my friend and spoke to us plainly.

"There are people in this place doing really bad illegal drugs. And this is where Jeff is. He has taken every penny we have and used it all to do drugs."

When she said this, I remembered earlier that week when Adrianne and I had asked her for some money for the ice cream truck.

"Hurry, hurry, he's gonna pass us!" we shouted, jumping up and down, while she had her hands in dishwater. She finally blurted out in a loud whisper, "Go to the encyclopedia and look under 'M,' on the page where it says money. There are some bills. Only take out two dollars. Close it up, make sure the money is all the way tucked in the pages, and put it back."

I marveled, excited by the little treasure hunt she sent us on. But now I understood why.

"We are not able to pay our rent," she went on. "I have to go in here, because he will not come home and I can't get ahold of him any other way. But I will be back. So do not get out of the car, no matter how long I am gone. Do you understand? I need you to stay with little Drew here in the car and help him go back to sleep if he wakes up. This is a very dangerous place."

Her eyes were swollen and bloodshot from crying, and we were shocked to see her this way. She was always so strong and in charge and felt like a safe place.

"Yes, ma'am," we answered, afraid, sad, angry, and confused. We were asleep when she finally came back. We never saw her husband again.

Fathers provide? This is what I knew of fathers. They didn't provide anything. They stole.

Father's Don't Correct, They Abuse

I thought about my best friend Amanda from high school. I thought about how her stepdad "corrected" us whenever he found out we were smoking weed.

"You're not allowed to smoke weed in this house," he said to us one night after her mom had left for work. "You can't smoke weed," he said, holding up his own bag of marijuana. "Until you drink this whole bottle of Goldschlager."

I remember finding out later that after we were too drunk and high to know what was going on, he would send me home and then sexually abuse Amanda. This kind of "correction" was a disgusting sham in order to please himself in the most despicable way.

What the Heck Is Water?

I had no idea what it meant to have a father, and I had no idea what it meant to have an orphan mentality. I didn't understand that my need to be a savior for myself and those around me was out of the feeling that no one else was trustworthy. Why did I need to be a savior? Because my experience taught me that, hey, you're on your own, girl. You want to be saved? Save yourself.

I heard a joke once that described how I felt about Eric's words: One fish asks another fish, "How's the water?" The other fish answers, "What the heck is water?" In the same way, since it was all I knew, I could not understand that I possessed an orphan mentality. And even if I could understand it, I would not have been able to see anything wrong with it. The truth is, street smarts are for the street, but in loving relationships they can be destructive. The brick walls around my heart were meant to keep bad things out, but when pure love asked to come in, the walls turned from protective to thieving. My "street smarts" turned into my own self-made prison that would keep true love out.

And so, Eric's whole presentation about God removing our orphan identity and our need to understand the heart of our heavenly Father toward us went right over my head. Later on, I realized this whole concept was central to my discovering my identity. I had always asked the questions:

"Is there a God or not?"

"Is God good or not?"

"Does he love me or not?"

"Is God all powerful or not?"

"Am I a blessing or a burden?"

"Am I alone or is he with me?"

And all of these questions were rooted in this one:

"Do I have a heavenly Father or am I an orphan?"

Eric later helped me realize that this question was the key to everything I needed for my spiritual, emotional, and (at suicidal times) physical survival.

Hero Note:
Tamy Elam

Meet Tamy Elam. She is a hero to me because
there are very few people I've met in my life
with a story like Tamy's who have uncovered
the healing power of *forgiveness*. She is gentle and
so powerful when she speaks. She is humble, but
her identity as God's royal daughter ignites a humbling,
honoring posture in the heart of those who hear her.

Here is a note to you, from Tamy.

Dear Reader,

God can take any broken heart and gently and
completely restore it. If I could go back to any moment
in my life, I would go back to that seven-year-old little
girl who cried herself to sleep at night. I'd say, your
heavenly Father is with you, listening to every prayer
you cry to him. There is punishment that is terrifying
for those who hurt innocent children, so you don't
need to try to punish your dad yourself. Pray that
the eyes of his heart would be willing to turn to your
heavenly Father in brokenness. He too can experience
the transformation you will one day receive. You have
a heavenly Father who loves you, with safe and perfect
love.

With the love of Christ,
Tamy Elam
wife, mom of six, writer, speaker

Sexual abuse is difficult to share because it violates the most intimate parts of you. It's unique in its sensual nature. It crosses sacred thresholds and enters into private places that are too personal to talk about. The Lord's powerful love crossed those thresholds that had been devastated in me from sexual abuse and made me pure, clean, whole, and free.

Tamy Elam

5

THE MYSTERY OF
a Father's Heart

For though you have countless guides in Christ, you
do not have many fathers.

1 Corinthians 4:15 ESV

I didn't realize it, but I had lost hope in fathers. Like a wounded animal, I began to expect pain from people. This is one of the tragedies of thinking like an orphan. I was always looking for someone to let me down. No matter what goodness was present, I would not trust it. Trust was something for fake people, those in safe homes on TV shows. The rest of us had to be smart enough to expect the worst. I was "getting wise." I had become an orphan without knowing it. I lost trust.

Without trust, you cannot receive love. Without the ability to receive love, you will wither away. I would have thrown this book across the room if I read the following words before I understood anything differently. But this is the truth: *women and men need each other.*

I would have spit in your face and said, "I don't need any man." But just because I have seen many men abuse their gifts doesn't change the fact that God created men and women each with a unique purpose and benefit to the world around them.

No matter the tragedies I've seen men cause, I have learned to value every human life. Now, instead of looking only for tragedy, I have learned to acknowledge that even the worst evil can be turned to amazing glory and goodness—and often is. We just need to have the hope and trust to look for it and see it. Most of the time we find whatever we look for. Many people don't want to forgive because they don't want to feel like they are excusing the wrong done to them. Forgiving someone does not mean "excusing" them. You must acknowledge the full weight of the crime in order to forgive. That can be deeply painful. It means mourning the loss of whatever was stolen as a result of the crime. But until we learn to forgive, we can't heal. And our insides will writhe and rage against even looking for anything good in whomever we have set our hatred against. This is a tragedy in so many ways, but the worst loss is the loss of a love that was intended to make us grow. And instead of growing we begin to wither and die.

God Wants to Teach Us How to Be Sons and Daughters

When I was sixteen, on the day God rescued me from suicide, a deacon in my grandma's church, Brother Partridge, prayed for me. He said, "God will be a better Father to you than any earthly father could ever be." My immediate thought was, *I don't need a dad.* Yes, I had problems. Yes, I needed something. But I could never have imagined the significance of having a father. I was raised by my mother, who never knew her father. My dad was in jail before

I ever remember meeting him. My great-aunt was a single mom with two children. Granny had been through a few bad marriages and now was married to a great man, but we weren't around him all the time. My friend's dads had only been trouble for them. I could not conceive how important fathers were.

When I asked Eric Patrick to be our band pastor, I imagined someone who would give us grand speeches, like the one he gave about revival the first time I met him, that would inspire us to do great things and not compromise the potential we had to change the world. I wanted him to give us a hands-off, Sunday service–type talk, once a week or so. I wanted to be more like his follower on social media and accept whatever I liked and leave whatever I wasn't interested in. I wanted to hear his brilliant thoughts, but I didn't realize I didn't really want him in my everyday life. Not because of him, but because of me. I never would have thought to ask him that, because I never imagined he would want that type of relationship. If he said he did, I would not have believed him. I didn't want to be that kind of burden on someone. But I didn't realize the depths of Eric's relationship with God.

Eric Patrick viewed God as his loving, heavenly Father. A real-life, ever-present, heavenly Father. Eric Patrick viewed himself as a child of God.

Eric would not be hired (even though we weren't paying him) to be a mere motivational speaker for five kids unless his heavenly Father made it clear that this was what Eric should be doing with his time and his relationship with us. When Eric set out to pray, he didn't ask God to do whatever he or we wanted. Eric prayed to his heavenly Father with an open heart,

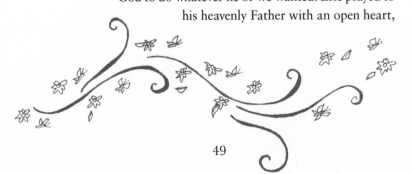

before a God he trusted and listened for. He searched the Scriptures. He searched for the peace of Christ to guide his own heart. He spoke with his own spiritual mentors. After all this, he waited until he understood the role that God was asking him to offer us.

God was asking Eric to offer us his heart as a spiritual father. Eric was obeying his heavenly Daddy. His Daddy said, *Eric, I want you to represent my heart to them. Represent to them what the heart of the Father is toward them. Show them how I love.*

Eric trusted God. It turns out that if you learn to be a good son, then you have the potential to be a great father. So Eric gave his heart over to five kids he barely knew, just in case they would ever respond to his offer, to represent the father-heart of God to them. It took me a long time before I responded to Eric's foreign words about taking away my orphan identity. It took a brush with death before I realized my deep need to understand the significance of a father in my life.

But at this moment in my life, my orphan identity was moving me into an unhealthy relationship with a married man. And I was blind to it.

Eric Patrick

Meet Eric Patrick. He is a hero to me for many reasons. One of the most powerful things in the life of someone with great responsibility and influence is for them to have pure motives. I have seen Eric through many different seasons over the past fifteen-plus years. Throughout it all he has taught me what purity looks like. His wisdom is gentle and miraculous.

Here is a note to you, from Eric.

Dear Reader,

We are a mist that appears for a little time and then vanishes, a ship sailing through the brief night. It is not up to us to determine the magnitude of the wake we leave. It is up to us to act justly, love mercy, and walk humbly with our God. He has made some vessels to leave small wakes and others to leave wakes felt thousands of miles away. When our journey is over, the only thing measured will be our relationship to him.

With the Father's love,

Eric Patrick

husband, father, pastor, business leader

———

The reward of walking with Jesus . . . is getting to walk with Jesus.

Eric Patrick

God is not a
prosecuting attorney
trying to win a case.

He is a judge who set me free.

6

The Mystery of
Our Deathly Freedom

For you have been called to live in freedom, my brothers and sisters. But don't use your freedom to satisfy your sinful nature. Instead, use your freedom to serve one another in love.

Paul the apostle, to the Galatian Christians[1]

You've been on the phone for hours, Lace," my friend Mel said. "Is everything okay?"

"Yeah, I'm just talking to Nathan. He is going through a lot right now."

"I bet. His wife's probably pretty pissed that he lives on the phone with another girl. But I'm sure he's happy to have you to talk him through this difficult time in his marriage," she said with her eyebrows high and a sarcastic smile.

"I know how it looks, but honestly it's hard to explain. I can't really talk about it."

"I'm sure you can't." She rolled her eyes and left the room.

I had several conversations like this with people I loved. And slowly, one by one, people I loved dropped out of my life. Although I should have seen this isolation as a warning sign, I took it the opposite way.

This was a response I'd learned from my "orphanness" too. I'd learned that when people didn't understand your loved ones, you protected them with your life. Orphans break the rules on purpose because they don't trust the rule maker. They feel the need to call the shots because they don't want to be controlled by what they perceive to be abusive authority. They feel as long as they are in control and are going against the mainstream then they are protecting themselves against getting tricked into a system they suspect is set up to take advantage of people.

This protective stance was how I responded whenever people like Mel challenged my relationship with Nathan. *She doesn't understand what he's going through. She doesn't understand what I've been through. And Nathan and I don't have to answer her questions.*

This destructive stance ultimately hurt those closest to me—those who cared the most for me.

God Will Fight for You, but He Will Not Fight You

One weekend the band was staying at Eric and Sarah's house. I could smell Italian herbs heating up in a steamy tomato sauce. Sarah must have been making a spaghetti dinner for all of us.

"Hey, Lace, who are you talking to?" Eric's voice and eyes were soft, safe, and not accusing at all when he asked me. Eric had met Nathan when he had come to my work a while ago. He saw how well we seemed to get along and had asked me a little about him.

I had told him that he was just a friend. That he was married, a Christian, and a good husband and father as far as I knew. That he went to church regularly and knew the Bible backward and forward and held on to Christ in order to stay sober. So when Eric asked who I was talking to, I answered honestly.

"Nathan Payne."

"Oh. Well, we're all gonna eat soon. Did you want to join us?"

"Yeah, Eric, hang on."

I walked back to the bathroom so I could talk privately. My phone conversation went on well past dinner. By the time I finally hung up the phone, everyone was getting ready to leave.

"Hey, Lace. Sorry we didn't get to see you at dinner."

"Yeah, sucks I had to miss it," I mumbled.

"What's going on?" Eric's eyes searched me.

"It's kind of personal, really," I answered.

Eric tilted his head, put his hands in his pockets, and said with genuine concern, "I was just thinking that if Nathan is having some problems, then maybe he should talk to another guy about them."

"You don't understand, Eric. He doesn't have anyone who understands him. I just prayed for him. He was just letting me know some of his situation and what he needs prayer for, and I can relate to a lot of what he is saying. I have similar struggles, and he prays for me and talks me through them and helps me. I know it seems like we talk a lot, but honestly all we ever talk about is Jesus."

"But do you think it's a wise decision to be talking to a guy who's married about your problems, one on one like that, all the time?"

"You're a guy who's married and I talk to you. What's the difference?"

Eric just looked at me and said nothing. I could tell he was worried, sad, brokenhearted, and feeling a little rejected. And I could sense he was backing off.

Your Heavenly Father Isn't a Prosecuting Attorney

I thought Eric was backing off because what I said made sense to him. I didn't realize it was because I was showing him that I was only trying to find holes in his questions so I wouldn't have to agree with his suggestion that talking to Nathan was inappropriate.

He was trying to make suggestions so I could come to my own conclusions. I, on the other hand, was trying to win an argument. Eric loved me too much to argue and fight with me. He would always fight *for* me, but never fight me. I figured if something was really wrong he would argue. I didn't understand the father-heart of God.

God the Father wants us to be free to make our own choice. He will suggest things but never change our minds with arguments or manipulation. God is not a prosecuting attorney trying to win a case. He is a judge who has set me free. With that freedom, I can choose to lock myself up in a prison if I decide to. Even if he suggests that it is not a wise choice, he will still let me make it because he honors and values my freedom. This is how Eric was loving me.

Later, I realized that I had hurt Eric in my resistance. But I didn't realize I was resisting him. I imagined he would arrest me in some way, that he would be forceful and yell and scream if he had to, to get me to wake up and realize the kind of death I was dancing with. I thought the rage and arguments I had experienced in my home growing up were the struggle of trying to make someone love you the way you needed to be loved.

I thought fighting *for* a person meant to *fight* the person if you had to. But fighting for someone and fighting someone are two very different things. Eric would never use angry intimidation to change my *no* to a *yes*. That's not how the father-heart of God loves us. In obedience to his heavenly Father, Eric had given me part of his heart as a spiritual father and let me break it.

Eric now reminds me that he and I talked a few times on the phone after this, and any time he mentioned Nathan I became defensive and angry. While I was writing this book, I spoke with Eric about that last conversation we had before I "ran away" from him and Sarah. He kept his eyes on Sarah's loving gaze of encouragement while tears flowed down his cheeks, and he recounted what he described as the most devastating moment of his time with Flyleaf.

"I remember exactly where I was, pacing back and forth when I called you. I said to you, 'Lacey, I am a warning sign right now, flashing lights at you, telling you the bridge is out, and you have to turn around.' And you said . . . " He paused, wiping away tears and fighting back more so he could continue. "You said, 'Eric, you're the devil right now speaking death over me. You're not for me, you've never been for me.'"

He kept his eyes on Sarah's still, unable to look at me. He seemed to be protecting my heart by avoiding eye contact, for fear I might feel accused or shamed, even though it was clear the thing that made him cry was rooted in his love for me as a daughter. He wiped more tears as we sat in silence for a moment, and then finished. "And then you hung up." The weight of his words hung in the air with a love I still have a hard time fathoming. I was amazed we ever reconciled enough for me to get to hear this story.

I don't remember this last phone call, but I'm certain what he recounted is true. I could not receive his gentle suggestions as a father. I didn't know what it meant to have a loving father I could trust regardless of if I agreed or understood what he was saying. So whenever I didn't understand, I didn't trust. And this was indeed the last time I spoke with Eric for many lonely, dark, confusing months.

Brian Welch

Meet Brian Welch. He is a hero to me because of his passionate love for life. He has been on many adventures all over the world. But his greatest love is for the God who changed his life. He brings the power and hope of heaven into places saturated with despair and hopelessness.

Here is a note to you, from Brian.

Dear Reader,

If I could write to my younger self, I'd write this to my twelve-year-old self: in the future, you're going to be given two cups to drink. The first drink will taste very sweet. You'll get everything you ever wanted and more. But there will be another cup you'll have to drink. This one will taste very sour and bitter. You will become someone you hate. You will encounter temptations that you will have no power to overcome. You will fall into a pit of despair and won't be able to climb out on your own.

But suddenly, like a truck going 80 mph on a freeway smacks a bug on its windshield—bam! Everything in your life will change in a blink of an eye. Love will awaken your heart for the first time. Not a love that fades, like the love of relationships you will ruin throughout your life. This is a love that won't die.

And it will give you a second chance. The person who gives this love is a laughingstock to many people, but you will know him as your EVERYTHING.

In the love of Christ,

Brian "Head" Welch
father, rock star, songwriter, author, speaker

It was like God and the Devil were fighting over my soul . . . a spiritual fight for my life, but it was up to me to make the final choice.

Brian "Head" Welch, *Save Me from Myself*

But the beauty
was a façade.

I began to fall
into
deception.

7

THE MYSTERY OF
Being Deceived

There are two ways to be fooled. One is to believe what isn't true; the other is to refuse to accept what is true.

Søren Kierkegaard[1]

One weekend my young little band got a gig on Sixth Street in Austin. This was such a big deal to us because until that time we had only played locally. We were one of two openers. The other was a band named Resident Hero. We became friends with them almost immediately. Shortly into my first conversation with Resident Hero's lead singer, Ryan White, I learned that we shared the same birthday. We also shared a love for music, grunge '90s honesty, and a past of being nerdy, bullied, passionate, and artistic. I was surprised to find that he also was a Christian.

Once we were talking about collaborating on one of his songs, and the conversation went to the topic of the Holy Spirit. I told him about how a long time ago I had prayed for the Holy Spirit to fill me and baptize me, like the Bible talks about, and I could tell something came to life in me. He asked me to pray for the same thing for him. So I did. The next day he called me out of the blue. He said he had a dream that night that bothered him. Most importantly, because of that dream he felt like he should give me a message.

"What is it?" I asked.

He seemed aware that it sounded crazy to say it, but I could tell the biggest burden he carried was to obey the strong sense he had to warn me.

"Beware of false prophets," he breathed at last.

Dreaming Up a Beautiful Lie

The very next day I was talking with Nathan when he said something I'll never forget.

"I had a dream," he announced. He was silent for an uncomfortable amount of time. He was good at these dramatic pauses. They made my mind race from the fantastic best to the most devastating worst. They made my stomach flip until I wanted to violently shake the answer out of him. Secretly, it got on my nerves. I didn't want to encourage this kind of drama, so I tried my best not to ask him what the dream was.

"What was the dream?" I eventually said, defeated.

"It was about us."

Dramatic pause.

He went on to explain that in the dream we were together in a romantic, sexual way.

I was shocked.

"I have to go," I said. I hung up before he had a chance to respond.

I watched the phone ring, thankful for its protection, flashing like my own personal lookout. *It's him! Run away!*

Ryan's words from the day before were ringing in my head like a noonday church bell. *Beware of false prophets.*

Finally, the phone stopped ringing.

I sat still in the quiet room, thinking about a million things. But what about all the ways Nathan had encouraged me? What about all the ways he spoke truth to me that helped me grow? What about how he seemed to know things he couldn't know about me? Weren't these all signs from God that he was safe? Weren't these meant to show me that Nathan Payne was, in many ways, a voice from God in my life? Couldn't I trust him? *Look at all these other things that are so good about our relationship,* I reasoned. *Haven't I gone through a divorce myself? Maybe his marriage was a mistake after all, like mine was. How can I judge him?*

But of course this was not the kind of thing that a godly man would say to a woman who is not his wife. Finally, I asked God a question.

"Was Nathan's dream from you, God?"

Yes. I felt his answer ring through my mind and throw it into confusion and fear.

The Heart Speaks in Metaphors

A couple of years ago, I was sitting in church one Sunday morning listening to my energetic seventy-year-old pastor speak to the congregation. I love that my pastor is in his seventies for many reasons. One of them is because he says what he says and doesn't care what anyone will think about it. His choice to be honest, instead of religious or politically correct like so many church people seem to be, makes me trust him a little more. He was talking about marriage and relationships and dreams. I was a little distracted because my two-year-old son, Jack, was trying to pry my phone out of my hands. But then my pastor said something that commanded my attention. I let go of the phone as my pastor's words resonated in my brain.

"When you get to the point in your relationship with your spouse where you can say, 'I dreamed I had sex with so and so' and they look at you and go, 'Well, what do you think it is, about so and so, that you need to connect within yourself? What does so and so represent to you, and how do you need to explore that in your own heart?' then you know that you are in a safe place with your spouse." I listened closer as he talked about the language of the heart.

"The heart doesn't speak in the English language. It speaks in pictures. It often speaks in metaphors." He went to on share how the Bible says that eternity is set in the hearts of people, and it speaks in earthly metaphors so you can understand the mysterious depths of eternity. He explained that sex in dreams can many times be a metaphor for closeness, intimacy, union, oneness, and knowing.

He also said people in dreams can sometimes represent ideas, concepts, or parts of ourselves we need to pay attention to. He went on about how God can speak to us in our dreams, but we often make mistakes when we interpret the message according to our own limited, earthly perspective or brokenness. This happens when someone feels like God has spoken to them to do or say something that totally goes against Scripture. That's why my pastor wanted to encourage us to study the Scriptures, and to spend time worshiping God in Spirit and in Truth, in order to understand God's character. He said that getting to know what God's heart is like through the Scriptures, taken in context through encountering love and holiness in worship, is pivotal to knowing what he would and wouldn't say to us personally.

We will easily get this wrong if we drift away from Scripture. God will never contradict himself. If it seems he is contradicting himself, it's time to be still and press in through more Scriptures, context, and prayer. Discuss it with godly people who love you, and look for God to show you how he is still cohesive.

I wish I had heard this sermon before I went through my divorce. But if I hadn't already gone through the pain of my ignorance by the time I heard it, I may have just kept on fighting with my two-year-old over the phone. It may have gone right over my head. This message took on living color as it brought up memories of some defining moments where I took the wrong direction in life and headed down paths of destructive deception.

Believing the False Prophet

I didn't speak to Nathan for a few hours. Then he texted me.

I really need to tell you something. It's important.

I couldn't ignore that like I probably should have. So I called him.

"I know this doesn't make perfect sense," he said as soon as he answered, "but I think God gave me the dream. The timing feels wrong, I know, but God is outside of time. I believe this is God comforting me because things are so bad at home. I believe you are a gift from God for me."

It sounded beautiful. It was like I got to be a *savior* for a man who needed me. But the beauty was a façade. I began to fall into deception. Even with the warning of him being a "false prophet," it was hard to reject the beauty of the offer. It was like he was saying, "Will you heal me like only you can?"

I didn't want to let him down, hurt him, or risk him hurting himself on his own without my help. It sounded so lovely to think God was giving us this relationship as a gift. But it was a beautiful, disgusting lie.

What God Was Not Saying

God was not telling Nathan that he and I were meant to be together in some parallel universe, that we would be together in the future and God would arrange it for us, or that we had married the wrong people and he was trying to fix our mistakes and let us know we were meant to be together.

If God was involved in the dream at all, whatever message God might want Nathan to take from it would have to line up with Scripture. It wouldn't go against the command not to covet. He would never tell me to desire to have what belonged to someone else. Nathan was another woman's husband. It was a rebellion against God's design for my heart and his purpose for my future to entertain a desire to have another woman's spouse for myself.

The Fruit of God's Holy Spirit

When the Holy Spirit of God leads a person to do something, the fruits that come out of Spirit-led action are written out in Scripture. Eugene Peterson paraphrases these verses in Galatians 5:22–23 like this:

> What happens when we live God's way? He brings gifts into our lives, much the same way that fruit appears in an orchard—things like affection for others, exuberance about life, serenity. We develop a willingness to stick with things, a sense of compassion in the heart, and a conviction that a basic holiness permeates things and people. We find ourselves involved in loyal commitments, not needing to force our way in life, able to marshal and direct our energies wisely. (Message)

The first most obvious fruit Nathan and I were missing was a willingness to stick with things, otherwise known as *faithfulness*. The next was an exuberance about life, or *goodness*. Then a sense

66

of compassion in our hearts, or *kindness*. If Nathan truly made the mistake of thinking God would tell him that we were meant to be together in the future, then that exposed his lack of *patience*—or not needing to force his way into my life—because he would have understood that telling me this while he was married to someone else was inappropriate. Nathan was not marshaling his feelings, emotions, or energies wisely. To do this equals *peace*. An emotional affair was not going to bring true peace to either of us.

And what about *joy*? Joy is a fruit of the Spirit that comes from hope in Christ's goodness and purpose despite the present circumstances. We would not get joy from having an emotional affair. It would be a selfish type of emotional pleasure at the expense of so many other people's pain and betrayal.

And, of course, this is not real *love*. It's more like the behavior of addicts who want what they think will make them feel good or happy in the moment no matter how fleeting it may be, what it costs, who it hurts, or how destructive it may be to themselves. And even when they know all of this, they either go to great lengths to justify it to themselves and others or find support groups of codependent people who will say what their ears are itching to hear. Or they will simply admit that it's all wrong and say they don't care anyway. Maybe getting help is too hard, so they don't try very hard to get it. But let me tell you, the effects of a destructive addiction are much harder to deal with than the effort, humility, money, time, and inconvenience of getting help.

Love is kind. Entering into a mental or emotional affair with someone was the opposite of kind. Love is not proud. And it was an ugly pride to think that it might be okay for me to consciously become part of breaking a covenant that two people made before God.

My orphan heart thought to love someone was to save them. I didn't understand the truth that the only person who can save someone is God.

My orphan heart thought to be loved by someone was for them to save me. I didn't understand that the only person who can save me is God.

My orphan heart thought love was to complete someone else and to be completed by them. I didn't understand that when two people who aren't whole try to complete each other they both end up with less than when they started. I didn't understand that the only one who can make a person whole is God.

I thought that love was to lay down my life for someone, no matter what. I didn't understand that if laying down my life caused both of us to die spiritually, emotionally, and relationally, then it's not benefiting me, them, or the world around us. That is not love; it's idolatry. It's enabling death and the destruction of both our souls and whoever we may touch by our death.

I thought romantic love was a mixture of extreme highs and lows. Abusing each other. Suffering for each other. Being both savior and leech to each other. Trapping each other and being addicted to the adrenaline of the cycle. I didn't realize that romantic love is meant to be a seal for a covenant marriage that, although may begin with passion, is only maintained by a consistent choice to love on purpose despite fickle feelings and fulfill the covenant vows.

I thought choosing to love in spite of your feelings looked like slavery and being fake and ignoring reality. I didn't realize that choosing love is being faithful to who you are beyond your fickle whims and feelings and circumstances. Choosing love is letting your *yes* really be yes and your *no* really be no. It's making yourself be honest with yourself and with your loved ones by keeping your words and keeping your heart commitments. It's choosing to keep loving when your heart tries to deceive you by telling you to run away from your promises once it gets difficult.

I thought love was forcing someone to stay, manipulating them by guilt, fighting them to be with you. Fighting with them to make them love

68

you. I didn't realize true love honors, values, and desires freedom. Love will honor your freedom to choose, honestly, what you really want. When that choice is destructive, as mine was, love continues to hope, as Eric did, that the beloved, wandering one will make it out alive and the story will turn to glory.

Hero Note:
Petra

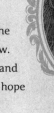

Meet Petra. She is a hero to me because she is the most honest Christ follower I know. She has a way of seeing life that is raw and poetic but filled with a passionate, fighting hope and faith.

Here is a note to you, from Petra.

Dear Reader,

If I could go back to my young self and give her advice I'd say, "Don't be afraid to forgive. I know you never learned to forgive anyone, not even yourself. All you know is how to fight back. but it never brings any peace, satisfaction, or healing at all. It only gets worse. You know why? because all your hate, anger, bitterness, and hurt forms into a whip in the hands of your worst enemy. This enemy is constantly hitting you with it over and over. As long as the whip is in the wrong hands, your wounds will never heal. but today you can disarm this enemy and end this. by starting to learn to forgive and receive forgiveness you will take the whip out of the hands of the enemy and hand it over to the only one who is able to handle the whip—Jesus. Remember the story where Jesus went into the temple angry, turning over tables? Remember when you heard this as a little girl, and how you wished you had someone like that Jesus who would fight for you like that? Even as a little girl you were already sick and tired of fighting, knowing you could never win this fight! You can decide what you want today. Do you want to live the rest of your life angry, bitter, and hurt, until you ruin everything—or do you want Jesus to help you and fight for you? Choose wisely!"

Love,
Petra
wife, mother, writer

8

THE MYSTERY OF
What Love Isn't

> Above all, don't lie to yourself. The man who lies to
> himself and listens to his own lie comes to a point that
> he cannot distinguish the truth within him, or around
> him, and so loses all respect for himself and for others.
> And having no respect he ceases to love.
>
> Fyodor Dostoyevsky[1]

After many long months of this roller-coaster relationship with Nathan, I found myself visiting a friend's church, but I don't remember anything the pastor said or who I met because the only thing I could focus on were the words painted around the edge of the ceiling. It was 1 Corinthians 13:4–7.

Love is patient.
Love is kind.
It does not envy.
It does not boast.
It is not proud.

It is not rude.
It is not self-seeking.
It is not easily angered.
It keeps no record of wrongs.
Love does not delight in evil but rejoices in the truth.
It always protects.
It always trusts.
It always hopes.
It always perseveres.

Over and over I read the words running around the edge of the ceiling. This is the way Scriptures are. They are like a mirror held up to us, showing us who we really are when we are deceived about ourselves. Little by little the words of this Scripture showed me my own heart.

I had lost love.

Over the past ten months I had become defensive. Angry. Selfish. Rude. Deceitful. Prideful. Unkind. Impatient.

As I looked at these verses, I thought about the first time a friend of mine questioned me about my relationship with Nathan and how I had responded defensively, like I was protecting him from other people.

"You don't understand what's going on. And it's not my place to tell anyone else about his business if he doesn't want anyone else to know." I went on to accuse her of being jealous and judgmental.

My friend looked hurt, but I felt like I had defended Nathan like a loyal friend should. I remembered my boss telling me to get off the phone at work and I responded by rolling my eyes, giving her the worst look of disgust. I remember her eyebrows raising

as if to say, "Who do you think you are?" I used to love my boss so much, and in order to defend my conversation with Nathan, who would not let me go sometimes because he "needed" me, I was rude to her. I had been so rude and had fought with almost everyone I loved around me over something to do with Nathan. I had been so chained to this needy relationship that I had alienated myself and had no one left around me.

I felt a deep darkness and depression following me everywhere. When I read the Scripture's definition of love on the ceiling of that church, I was reminded of Jesus. I missed him. It showed me how far away I had drifted from him. It revealed how horrible I was without him in my life.

True Love Exposes Imposters

After that service, I walked to my car. Before I opened my door I turned my phone back on (I had turned it off for the service). I had dozens of texts from Nathan.

> Why aren't you answering my calls?

> I need to talk to you now.

> Are you with someone else?

> I can't believe you're doing this to me.

On and on the messages went. Before I could dial his number my phone was ringing.

"I'm sorry," I greeted him immediately with an apology.

"You're sorry? Really? How could you say you're sorry when you haven't responded to me for over two hours of me trying to get ahold of you? I have done so much for you, given up so many things for you, and you can't even answer your phone? You did the same thing to me last week when you were with your family. Do you even know

74

what is happening with my family right now? I'm going through hell at home for you. You owe it to me to at least answer your phone."

"I turned my phone off because I was in church."

"You turned your phone off? How could you turn off your phone when you know what I have been going through?"

He was angry, and I felt glad that I wasn't with him or I would have been scared.

"I'm sorry," I said again.

"Listen to me. Don't ever do that to me again."

His voice was shaking like he was in tears. But with every word he spoke, the Scripture was scrolling through my mind.

"I need you to answer when I call."

Love is patient. Kind.

"I'm dealing with a lot right now and I can't handle it without you."

It isn't jealous, boastful, proud, rude, or self-seeking.

"Please make sure you are there for me because without you I can't make it."

It is not easily angered and keeps no record of wrongs. Love does not delight in evil but rejoices in the truth.

"I love you. Don't you realize that?"

It always protects.

Always trusts.

Always hopes.

Always perseveres.

I could recognize physical and sexual abuse. I could recognize when someone I knew and loved was being emotionally abused. But I couldn't recognize it when it was happening to me. The Scriptures reminded me of all the ways that love had been perverted in my life and in the lives of those I loved. But emotional abuse wasn't the worst wrong in our relationship; it was the fact we both exalted our "love" above God. I had called so many things love that, after reading this Scripture, seemed to be so completely unlike the love of God.

Fiona DesFontaine

Meet Fiona DesFontaine. She is a hero to me because her life carries the fragrance of grace and truth in the most profound ways. Her depth of knowledge, understanding, and love have impacted me forever. Her testimony reminds me that God is all powerful. It calls for reverence and wonder toward the most powerful God who truly loves us all.

Here is a note to you, from Fiona.

Dear Reader,

Two of the most important things that you can understand in life are freedom and eternity.

Jesus came to set us free so that we can walk in truth and freedom. In doing so, we can open blind eyes and set captives free. We have to love truth and hate lies. The bible is the source of all truth, so learn to love the scriptures as the word of God.

Colossians 3:1–4 is a scripture I live by. We are to set our hearts and minds on heaven.

Ecclesiastes 3:11 tells us that God has set eternity in the hearts of people. You are created for eternity.

If I could give my younger self advice, I would go back to age fourteen. At this age I began to be sexually molested by a man who would control my life through a combination of anger, bullying, threats, and doing shameful things to me. I would tell my fourteen-year-old self not to allow myself to be overpowered and subjected to anyone else's desires, threats, rages, or jealousy. I would tell that young girl that no one has the power to trap her or force her into a nightmare existence.

I would tell her to speak up, to tell someone what her abuser was doing, and to realize that silence and secrecy enable her abuser to lock the doors of her prison. I would tell her that self-respect is critical, because her body, soul, and spirit are hers alone, to be used to glorify her Creator. No human has the right to destroy our self-respect.

Love,

Fiona DesFontaine
mother, pastor of His Church in Durban,
South Africa, speaker

———

The babiest Christian with one Scripture in their mouth can overcome all the powers of hell.

Fiona DesFontaine

That's how good liars are—

setting their lies down in a pool of truth so you dismiss the lie in the middle because of the truth surrounding it.

9

THE MYSTERY OF
Freedom and Suicide

The greatest hazard of all, losing the self, can occur very quietly in the world, as if it were nothing at all. No other loss can occur so quietly.

Søren Kierkegaard[1]

*T*he hotel was a cheap one. By now, my boss and coworkers were probably wondering where I was. I wasn't sure if I would have a job when I got back, but I didn't care. The flight to Colorado from Texas was last-minute and expensive. My excuse for this trip was that I was meeting Robb Kelley, a sort of spiritual granddad. Eric Patrick called him his own spiritual papa. He had always been kind to me, and since I had not spoken to Eric Patrick in so long, I thought maybe it would be good to talk to Robb.

The truth was, I was ready for change. Change *had* to come. The days kept coming and time wouldn't stand still, go backward, or fast-forward. So I knew, whether I was ready or not, change was the thing that was suffocating me. I had to give in.

Nathan was also there, ready to meet me. He had a busy weekend working in Colorado for his new job with a timeshare company, but he said he would make some time to see me.

The way I saw it, I had three choices before me.

One, I could leave *with* Nathan.

Two, I could leave him.

Or three, I could die.

Dying for my convictions had been one of the chief objectives of my life ever since I was a little girl. I always found the idea to be so heroic.

On this day, my problem was that I faced two convictions I was ready to die for: dying for someone else to be saved or dying for my faith.

I felt like if I consented to turning this emotional affair into a full-blown physical one where we ran away—Nathan leaving his wife and children and me leaving my life as well—then I would be added to the large group of people who make up the list of reasons why so many say they hate Jesus. People like my teenage atheist self, waiting to blame Jesus for the bad things Christians do.

But I also felt that if I didn't consent to the affair then I would be contributing to the death of a severely wounded and needy man, whom I thought I was keeping alive by loving him.

So I met him at this cheap hotel. He sat in the corner of the room and could only give me a few minutes of his time. I sat on the ugly floral print–covered bed. I didn't say much.

He explained the reasons why he needed me to keep loving him. How he couldn't live without me. How I was such a healing part of his life. Then he explained why he couldn't leave his wife and children. Next he taunted me about his desire to run away together. Then he came back to the fact that he didn't see how we could do it just yet. And lastly he spoke about something else that he couldn't have known was in my heart, the way he often did, pulling out my deepest held secret thoughts and talking about them like he knew me better than I knew myself. This special ability was the most confusing part about him, because it made me want to let this part of our talk validate all the other confusing parts of the conversation. The things I wasn't sure about must be true if this part was so obviously true.

That's how good liars are—setting their lies down in a pool of truth so you dismiss the lie in the middle because of the truth surrounding it. Good liars also work really hard to make themselves believe what they are saying. They make conscious decisions to believe the lies they are creating. This is why it is so hard for them to recognize truth if it is something they don't want to believe. "Truth" ends up being reduced to whatever the liar wants to believe, regardless of its veracity. Liars are just sick, that's all, and they need healing like we all do. They need to be made whole instead of dividing themselves up with lies.

After he made his last chill-inducing, how-could-you-know-that-about-me point, I immediately thought of the phrase Ryan had said to me. *Beware of false prophets.*

Then we sat in silence for a while. I loved this man. I wanted him to use his amazing gifts for all that God intended them to be used for. I wanted him to be well, healthy, full of joy, truth, and freedom. I saw how much love God had for him as well. I didn't know how I could hurt him and risk his words being true: "I need you or I can't keep going another day."

At the same time, I knew that I couldn't risk dragging Jesus's name through the mud, giving skeptics like my young atheist self another reason to mock the name of Jesus. So we sat in a heavy silence until he left me alone in the room.

Life or Suicide?

I called Robb Kelley but he didn't pick up. I had left him a message, but he still hadn't called back.

All I could think of, while I sat alone in this cheap hotel on that ugly bed, was the pink razor that lay on the edge of the bathtub. I wondered how hard it would be to take apart. Our thoughts can create our reality. As I thought through wanting to die rather than hurt Nathan by leaving, and wanting to die rather than misrepresent Christ by being in an affair, the only thing that made sense to me was to kill myself.

It's funny what "making sense" means in times when we are deceived, confused, and oppressed by suicidal demons. Suicide didn't really make sense. For a Christian, it spits in the face of the God who made you and gave you another day for a reason that you may or may not see. As I look back on this time, I think about that mysterious verse where Jesus talks about demons. He said that when a demon is cast out of a person, it goes through arid regions looking for a place to rest. If it can't find a new place to inhabit, it returns to the place from where it was cast. If that place is swept clean and in order, but unoccupied, then it comes back and brings seven more demons more terrible than itself, and the condition of that person is worse than before (see Matt. 12:43–45).

This is a mysterious verse that I don't fully understand, but what seems clear from my experience is that *suicide* is most likely the name of a demon that torments people and tries to convince them to kill themselves. I am very familiar with this sort of torment, and many times can even sense when someone else is struggling with it. I also know that on that day at the hotel, while I was alone for that little while, I was closer to suicide then than I ever was at age sixteen, or any time after that.

Just as I was about to go get the razor, the phone rang.

I looked at it for a few seconds and let it ring, wondering if I should answer or continue with what I was doing.

I wanted it to be Robb, but what if it was Nathan?

For no reason I could understand, I picked up the phone almost while I was still wondering if I should.

I didn't speak for a minute, but then I heard his voice.

It was Robb.

"Hello? Lacey, are you there?"

Tears fell from my eyes as I answered his strange question, not sure if it was really true.

"Yes, I'm here."

"We got your message, Lacey. My wife, Shiloh, and I are on our way. It will take us about an hour to get there, but we wanted to let you know that we will be there soon."

I knew I would wait for them. It was like God himself had called to interrupt my plans. I love that he uses people to do great, seemingly impossible things in the lives of others. That must be one of God's greatest joys—to call other people who will say yes to him, to help intervene in miraculous ways at just the right moments in other people's lives. Oh, if only we would all listen and obey when he nudges us to do out of the ordinary, loving things.

I just sat there while I waited, swinging back and forth from being overwhelmed and crying to feeling completely numb and empty.

A Father's Love

When Robb and Shiloh finally arrived, they both gave me particularly long, extra-tight hugs. It made me feel awkward how they displayed their love for me, like I was a daughter. Our relationship felt sort of random and yet they seemed to view me like I was a precious family member. I had never done anything to benefit them and they really had nothing certain to gain from dropping everything to drive an hour out of their way to a crummy hotel to maybe talk some sense into me—especially when I'd been known to be gifted with the ability to reason my way in or out of whatever I wanted, no matter how right or wrong it was. I didn't understand this was how fathers treated their daughters.

Fathers provide presence.

But when you are honestly ready to die, I think there is something about everything you are, and know, and are used to, being really fragile. In this moment it only took one conversation to break apart my default settings so that I could really hear.

I didn't know where to start with Robb. As weird as it sounds, I wanted to respect Nathan's wife by not sharing too much of what was going on. I vaguely told him some of the story and asked a question about not knowing whether what you heard in your heart was really from God.

That's when Robb began telling me his story.

Fathers provide wisdom.

He talked about how he met a woman who seemed to have the same type of spiritual gifts as him. When Robb first spoke with her, she would light up in amazement at how well he seemed to understand her heart. Robb felt the same way when she spoke to him. She would pull out the deepest secret truths of his heart.

"We made the mistake of thinking that because we connected so deeply spiritually, it must be a sign from God that we were meant to be together romantically," he said.

Later he realized that the relationship was destructive in many ways and was able to salvage their hearts by ending it. I had never considered this before. It flew in the face of everything pop culture taught me about following your heart and recognizing "true love" in romance. Pop culture taught me the main purpose of life was to find your soul mate. Pop culture taught me that I would recognize this person by how we connected in our souls. It didn't matter what gender, race, or circumstance the person came from either. If your true love was romantically involved with, or even married to, someone else, that was simply a plot to overcome in this great love story before you got your happily ever after.

Pop culture has glorified coveting. Pop culture has painted a desire for someone who is not yours into the beginnings of a grand love story. In reality, this is not love at all. It's theft.

It's deceiving yourself.

It's idolatry.

It's adultery.

It's our orphan fear that God doesn't have something good for each of us in mind.

It's pride and greed, wanting something that isn't yours to have.

It's exchanging real pearls for fake ones that won't last. We yearn for it, because it masquerades as the true love we need from heaven. But when the mask comes off, we realize that true love is not who we are dancing with. There is a faint voice at our backs whispering truth to our hearts.

Following your feelings has deceived you.

Looking for a soul mate has taught you to chase the wind.

True love is not a wind that deceives and disappears.

Love Speaking Truth

I was so thankful that Robb could speak truth to me out loud. It was a heart-wrenching relief to come to the understanding that just because we could connect deeply on a spiritual and emotional level did not mean that Nathan and I were meant to be together romantically.

When Robb spoke, something shifted in my heart. I understood that what he explained was exactly what had brought so much confusion in regard to this married man I was involved with. It was confusing for both of us, and Robb's story helped explain why. If we had looked at our connection as a mere marvel from God, because of how he freely gifts people, we would have understood our connection differently.

It would have been an encouragement to know that God made others who share our passions and see life similarly. We wouldn't have filtered our similarities through pop culture romance and began to covet romantically in our hearts what was not ours to have. We would have understood that we were simply a brother and sister in Christ. And we actually would have appreciated each other in *appropriate* ways.

I sensed such a light enter the room that I felt peaceful and hopeful. Then the phone rang again. It could only be one person. I didn't know what I should do, and Robb encouraged me to go ahead and answer. I don't remember our conversation, but as we talked, the cloud that was over my heart before seemed to return. When I hung up, Robb pointed that out.

"I want you to acknowledge what just happened. There was peace here before, and now there is a darkness in the room. Do you sense that?"

I did.

"I want you to see that there is no life in this relationship, and you must trust God in order to receive the life he wants to give you. If you don't trust God, you will end up with counterfeit versions of life that only look good for a short while. Once you get into that place of resisting God's best for your life, you will find strife and struggle and hardship you were never meant to face."

Fathers protect and correct.

It was then that I remembered an email my friend Victoria had sent me before I even met Nathan. I thought the email was strange and had no idea what it meant, really, when I read it. This was the first time I'd thought about it since she'd sent it over a year ago. It read:

I had a dream that you were in a broken down, dirty trailer house, and you were with a man. In my dream it was as if he was your husband. . . . You were sitting on the edge of a bathtub and you were staring at a string of pearls that were hanging over the edge of the tub. When I saw you, I knew that you were being abused in this relationship.

When I looked closer at the pearls, I could see they were really cheap costume jewelry pearls and they were chipped and faded. When I woke up I felt like God was saying that this doesn't have to be your future because he says he has true pearls for you and such blessing you can't even imagine.

As I remembered this email from my prophetic friend, I wept. In my heart, I asked God to forgive me and to help me find a way out of all of this darkness I didn't know how to escape. Robb and Shiloh prayed for me. Shortly after, they left. I ended up using the return flight I previously did not expect to use and went home.

God Speaking

I arrived late that night and my roommate Melanie was still up, sitting in the kitchen when I walked in. She had been trying to connect with me because she knew I was struggling with depression lately. But I didn't answer her calls. I had been rude to her and she had loved me all along anyway. She gave me a quick hug and then looked me over in a strange way.

"How are you doing?" she asked.

"I'm better, I think."

"I had all my church pray for you yesterday."

"Why?"

"Because I had a vision of you. I saw you sitting in a hotel room on a bed with a floral print, and you were really sad. You were thinking about the pink razor that was sitting on the edge of the bathtub and you were planning to take it apart."

I began to sob.

I was so amazed that God would speak to Melanie to pray for me. I was amazed that she would say yes to God's invitation to pray for me. And not only her, but she asked others to pray. I was astonished at how much God loved me. It is phenomenal how personal and specific he can be in the way that he loves.

That night I opened Mel's Bible and read Proverbs 5–7. It was another mirror. It felt like I was reading everything I was going through with this emotional affair. I wept and wept and prayed. But when I prayed I felt so empty and lost. It felt like I had pushed God a million miles away and didn't know how to get back to the place where I could sense his love for me.

It took me some time to understand that it is impossible to push God away. We turn our backs on him. We forget about him. We deal badly with him. But he does not leave us. He does not betray us. The poet-writer of the psalms writes, "If I make my bed in the depths, you are there" (Ps. 139:8). We can turn from him but he stays with us. He follows us into the blackness, waiting for us to reach out and grab hold.

Melanie Savoie

Meet Melanie Savoie. She is a hero to me because, as I described in this chapter, she is such a faithful listener. For ten years she toured as my stylist and prayer warrior while I was in Flyleaf. She wars for truth by constantly keeping an open dialogue with God in her heart. Her devotion to hearing and obeying God's voice has saved many lives. Her prayers have been filled with some of the most powerful displays of God's love I have ever encountered in my life.

Here is a note to you, from Melanie.

Dear Reader,

When I was young, I thought there was no other way to live except the ways the world bombarded me with. I thought all the destruction I saw was just life. But the truth I've learned is: life doesn't have to be like that. God can use our mistakes and turn them into glory.

If I could, I would go back to age nineteen and tell myself to slow down and face my problems. I would encourage myself to really listen to what God is saying and understand his words. I would tell myself to find God's way because it is the best way. I would tell myself to not give my body away before marriage, because it wouldn't bring the love I longed for, only the opposite.

With the love of Christ,

Melanie Savoie, CNA
stylist, intercessor, speaker

God asked me to go on a half-hour drive with a man who had abused me. I didn't want to go, but I couldn't ignore God. By the end of the drive, I was praying with this broken man for Jesus to forgive him and be the Lord of his life.

Melanie Savoie, "Whosoever Testimony CD"

10

THE MYSTERY OF
Rage and Questions

A gentle touch of the brush on the canvas
A forceful blow in earth's mine
A thin line hidden in a mighty oak
A faint cry of a mother in labor
A rising star in the dark sky of the mind
A never felt current in the deep of the heart

Andrea Danko, "Change"[1]

Sometimes the hardest part of spiritual healing lies in the moment when truth is realized. Truth brings its own hammer. It smashes deception. It pounds lies. The hammer of truth was upon me now. It had been weeks since I saw Nathan in the hotel; each week added more weight to my slumping heart. Finally, the pounding of truth's hammer came upon my body, mind, and soul.

The Gagging and Heaving of Righteous Anger

It was impossible not to think of Nathan. Everywhere I turned were reminders. Triggers. I looked up at the stars. They seemed like the only thing I had left that wasn't tainted. As if God protected the stars, to keep them for me and him. The worst part of living with my friend Mel was there was no way to climb onto the roof of her house. The rage washing over me was something I hadn't felt since I was sixteen. I had no present coping mechanism for dealing with it. Somehow the neurons in my brain found a very old rut to ignite, and I wanted drugs and a roof to lie on while I did them. But even back then, even if I had no drugs, my refuge was the roof.

I remember the day I met the God I didn't believe in. As I stood before him, my life flashed before my eyes and I saw those moments of searching on the roof. I knew in that moment of encountering God that even when I called the Texas sky a faithful friend it was really God who was calling me up to be with him and to be still.

I thought about driving to a different neighborhood with roofs I could climb on. What if I got arrested for climbing on someone else's roof? That would be a new adventure to interrupt my rage and sadness . . . and I wouldn't care.

But the longer I laid on the cold grass in my backyard, looking up at the stars, the more I sunk into the debris of my own heart. I saw a mosquito land on my arm out of my peripheral vision. I could feel the grass move slightly against my bare toes. Was a bug crawling on me? My heart and mind were too heavy and busy for

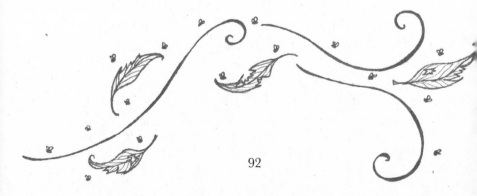

me to find out. I was too engaged to spend one ounce of energy to move or care.

I let the mosquito drink. I let the bug explore. They owned the dirt, right? And this body was only a moment or a century away from becoming dirt anyway. This body wasn't really me. I left it on the cold grass while I ventured into my soul. The more I saw, the more I broke. The more I remembered, the more I worried that vomiting would take over my body and interrupt my focus as I tried to sort through all this madness—sadness, anger, betrayal, deception, violation of all that I knew I was. The physical body I was living in was agreeing with my brokenness and sense of injustice to the point of making poetic metaphors.

It wanted to throw up.

You have ingested poison!

She was warning me.

Here let me help you get it out before it kills you!

Calm down, body, I said to the drama queen, annoyed. *The poison is in my heart, not my stomach. I'm trying to get to the bottom of this. If you leave me alone, maybe I can just think and figure this out. Puking won't help anything.*

I made myself breathe slowly. Closing my eyes, I replayed my last encounter with Nathan. I held the sounds, images, and feelings of it out in front of me with open hands and an open mind. I sought to see the truth of the scene without any filters. I needed clarity. I needed objectivity. I wanted truth in my innermost being.

"I'm not going to do this anymore. I've asked you to stop calling me, and yet you keep calling. I will be changing my number," I'd said firmly, as my heart threatened to beat out of my chest.

"I need you. I don't know if I can live without you. I don't know if I will. How can you do this to me right now?"

These words sat on top of the past ten months. I scanned the memories of those months. Each one was like a brick in the thick wall around my heart. I saw and felt his last few sentences block out any light or air I had been living on. They were like an iron cage, meant to seal off the top of the tower I was locked away in. His words were the fire of a dragon threatening to kill me if I tried to escape.

And I saw the lies. The mortar used to hold the bricks together were lies. I only needed to push the wall and watch the whole tower fall. Memory by memory, brick by brick, I pushed and saw the lies exposed. As the bricks fell, I felt rage mounting in me. I felt wounds bleeding. The rage was so strong I didn't feel pain, just anger.

He used me.

He humiliated me.

He bullied me.

He perverted all the good things in me.

He turned me into a drug to replace his addiction, to abuse in whatever way felt good to him. And with all the good things in me perverted, I could find nothing good left in me. Only rage.

My Violent Rage

Before I realized what was happening, I was off the lawn and slamming open the door to the storage shed where my friend had let me keep my things. There was my innocent bookshelf covered in CDs. I screamed as I pulled the heavy thing away from the wall and threw it on its face. I picked up every CD case I could find and smashed it against the wall. I crushed them under my bare feet. I moved on to break anything around that could be broken.

When I could find nothing else to break, I wept. I sat in the mess, realizing the metaphor my body had sought out without my even knowing what had happened. Yes, his perversion of everything good in me had ravaged my soul. But in many ways I had allowed it, and in many ways I had done it to myself. How? Why?

I sat in my garage with bloody hands and feet and wept to see in myself a metaphor for my own heart. I walked into the house, tracking blood through the kitchen, into the back room where I slept, and I crawled under my sheets and fell asleep. It had been so long since I fell asleep crying. I remembered the words of the man who stopped at the door of the church so many years ago to let me know that God saw me when I cried myself to sleep at night.

Did he see me now? Maybe so. Maybe not. I wasn't sure anymore.

I held my breath as if I was putting my life on pause somehow.

11

The Mystery of
Memories

Blessed is the man who endures temptation, for when
he has been approved, he will receive the crown of life
promised to those who love him.

James 1:12 WEB

*T*he sun crept through my window. Its light nudged me. My
feet and hands throbbed from last night's angry rampage in
the garage, smashing CD cases. I was waking up.

Oh, no.

I laid there, hearing nothing but my own heartbeat.

I held my breath.

My heart beat louder.

Mel was already at work and I was alone. The anxiety of waking
up to the quiet house, with nothing to do but remember, brought
on a childish attempt to stop something I couldn't really control.

I held my breath as if I was putting my life on pause somehow. But no. The sun was still moving, changing the light in my room, making it brighter. I wasn't ready for another day yet. The sunlight lit up my eyelids, and I saw colors swirling behind them, triggering a memory without my consent.

"What are you doing?" I asked him as he sat silent and still, with his head tipped back against the wall, eyes closed, tilting his face toward the light on the ceiling.

"I'm watching the colors swirl behind my eyelids."

"When you try and focus on one, does it float away from you, and more come swirling in from the other side of your eyes?" I smiled.

His eyes popped open, still staring at the ceiling. "Yes." He blinked.

"It's like a game," we said in unison.

I laughed. He turned his head toward me without a smile, looking much more serious than I understood.

"People usually make fun of me and ask what I'm smoking whenever I tell them I see swirling colors behind my eyelids."

He searched me the way he did so often when he was trying to communicate something deeper than he had words for, or something he wasn't sure he should speak out loud. This time he explored my eyes with a compassionate sorrow, like he was wondering if I felt alone like him and was desperately hoping I needed a friend too.

I did.

All My Hateful Memories

A growling scream started in my belly and poured out of my mouth as I finally exhaled and shouted with my whole soul, "Go away!" The words sliced violently into the silent air of my empty house. Tears streamed down the sides of my face, pooling into my ears.

I couldn't even close my eyes and rest, alone. The memories invaded the deepest parts of me.

I pulled the sheet over my head and opened my eyes, thinking I could hide from the memories by keeping them open. But my breath was so much louder under the covers. I remembered this spot. I remembered this sound. I remembered.

I held the phone away from my mouth so my loud breath didn't drown out his voice. Burying my head under covers was sometimes my only way to get any privacy in the noisy house when Mel had friends and family over. So I kept my head under here when we talked.

"It got quiet. Where did you go?" he asked me.

"Neverland. I'm on Mermaid Lagoon."

He laughed. "Ah. You know it's not safe for mortals to be there at night."

He always met me in my whimsy and never let it slip past him.

"We aren't mortals though, right?" I answered.

"True, I only mention it so that if you run into any mortals you can warn them."

"Or I could turn them into one of our kind."

"Yes!" he said. "You could tell them the story of how Peter laid down his life to save Wendy on that very lagoon."

I never had to explain what I meant when I made inferences to Jesus without mentioning his name.

"I don't remember that from the movie," I realized out loud.

"It's from the book. He sent her away on a kite so she wouldn't drown. Then as he prepared himself to die, he smiled about how death would be a great adventure."

"Isn't that the most freeing thing about Jesus?" I mused. "We lose our fear of death. Before I knew Jesus I would've said I wasn't afraid to die, but that's only because I didn't know what I was saying or contemplating, when I thought about death. But after I met Jesus I not only was ready to die but also willing and excited to live."

"Hmm." *He considered this and paused, as he often did, before pouring warm words into my heart. "'Man cannot possess anything as long as he fears death. But to him who does not fear it, everything belongs. If there was no suffering, man would not know his limits, would not know himself.'"*

"Is that Peter Pan?" *I wondered.*

"It's Tolstoy." *I could hear him smiling as he corrected me.*

"I need a kite like the one that carried Wendy away," *I confessed.*

"Me too," *he agreed.*

Uncoiled and Falling

My second guttural scream was full of anguish. I covered my face with a pillow, as if I could hide the fact that it hurt so deeply from my own ears.

"Shut up!"

My muffled cry came and I wept with deep sobs that drove me out of bed to the floor where I could rest my head against the wall above the trashcan in case I threw up.

I was trying to look into the trashcan to see if it was empty as a wave of nausea hit me. But instead of focusing on the trashcan, all I could see were tears clinging to my lashes with my heavy eyes barely open. The light of the sun hit them and rainbows shot out like rays of sunlight, triggering another memory.

"Rainbows are so magical," *he said, looking into his water glass.*

"I haven't seen many in my life," *I mused.*

"They're everywhere. Anywhere there is water and light. Look in your glass."

I did. I couldn't see any rainbow at first, but I trusted him. He was so sure of himself when he said odd things like this. He lived every moment like he was in a different world than everyone else. The world he lived in was filled with immense, unfathomable mystery. I always believed him first and doubted him later. But he

*was brave enough to speak of things I was only constantly rest-
less over not being able to put words to . . . things I knew and
sensed but felt alone in, because speaking them would make those
around me get quiet and withdraw and start asking, "When's
lunch?" But he seemed to choose to be mocked rather than let
something magical be overlooked. He was always pointing out
beauty, mystery, and the mystical nature in everything. So I trusted
him and searched for the colors in my water. I began to see them
and laughed.*

"Yes. *There are rainbows in my glass. It is sort of magical, huh?"*

"Well, *I only use 'magic' as a word to describe something nu-
minous, something we don't fully understand, something we only
catch a glimpse of—its weight and beauty and glory. It feels supernatural to us and from another realm, like heaven. The Bible
says that a rainbow encircles the throne of God. So anytime I see
rainbows in light and water or glass, I think of the throne of God
being among us.*

"Do *you realize our bodies are made up of ninety percent water?
And what does the Bible call Jesus in John chapter one? The 'light.'
His light shining though us makes a rainbow, but the rainbows
we can see are only one shallow dimension of what colors are in
heaven. In heaven they are fragrant and sing and dance and carry
knowledge. This is why we shine when he lives in us. This is what
we are made for. We are made to be thrones for God."*

Threaten Me

He spoke so easily about things I had written about with such
awe and caution in my journals. I didn't know how to say these
things that he was putting words to so quickly. But I knew they
were true. I'd written about it only a few weeks ago. *How does he
do that? How does he talk about things that he can't know that I
have been thinking about? How does he know the longing in my*

101

heart better than I know it myself? And then he would go on to challenge that longing and make it grow.

"Oh, God," I said, as I watched my tears begin to fall into the trashcan. "Help me. How do I live? How do I think? How do I move on? How do I look at anything or think of anything? This person is everywhere!"

Silence.

Stephana Mosley

Meet Stephana Mosley, who happens to be my little sister. She is a hero to me because of the way she fights for her heart to belong to Jesus alone. After experiencing the pain of giving her heart away to people and things that weren't God, she learned the glory of setting her heart aside for the Lord and shines with the faith she carries and the depth of her love for him.

Here is a letter to you, from Stephana.

Dear Reader,

When I was younger, I identified myself in so many ways that had nothing to do with who I was. It brought so much confusion and emptiness to my heart. When I finally understood that I could learn who I really am through what God says about me I found such peace, hope, and healing. God's love for me and plan for me is filled with life beyond anything I could dream.

If I could go back to age fourteen, I would tell myself what it means to guard my heart. I would tell myself not to give my body away. I would tell myself that God has a wonderful plan to do great things in my life. I would tell myself not to miss the joy and freedom of allowing everything to unfold in his timing.

With true love,
Stephana Mosley
musician, songwriter

Let me show you how to love. I promise you it's safe. There's no one else with a heart like yours. Don't throw that away. Keep it safe.

Stephana Mosley, "Safe"

PART 2

FINDING TRUE LOVE

Your love's not fractured
It's not a troubled mind
It isn't anxious
It's not the restless kind
Your love's not passive
It's never disengaged
It's always present
It hangs on every word we say
Love keeps its promises
It keeps its word
It honors what's sacred
Cause its vows are good
Your love's not broken
It's not insecure
Your love's not selfish
Your love is pure
You don't give your heart in pieces
You don't hide yourself to tease us

Amanda Cook, "Pieces"[1]

12

The Mystery of
Silence

"I hid my face from you for a moment, but with ever-lasting kindness I will have compassion on you," says the LORD your Redeemer.

Isaiah 54:8

*S*ilence from God is the loudest and saddest thing I've ever heard. This kind of deep silence followed every prayer I had prayed for the past six months. God's silence was the darkest feeling of all that I was facing inside. It was in these excruciatingly quiet moments that I began to wonder about God.

And the devil was always at my heels, giving me answers to my sad questions.

Wasn't it God who told you this affair was a gift to you both from him? The same voice that told you were saved in the first place? And if he was wrong about this person who keeps hurting you, then maybe he was wrong about your salvation. Maybe he never spoke to you at all. Maybe you just made it all up in your head to begin with. There is no way for you to know anymore. There is no knowing anything at all anymore.

In the midst of this doubt I thought of my first promise ring. I thought of the way I used to turn it around on my ring finger so only the smooth part of the band showed. Then I would tell the customers I waited on at Shoney's I was married if they asked.

"Yes. I'm married to Jesus."

They would either look confused or horrified at my answer. It used to make me laugh. I didn't care what they thought. My heart began to burn when I thought about Jesus. It ached. I missed him so desperately. I thought about how being "married to Jesus" was a good way to explain how lovesick and committed I was to God.

I had made so many "forever" statements in worship about my commitment to God. I thought about those worship songs I used to sing to him. I began to hear them in my head and started to cry as I sang them softly through my sobs.

I had to make a choice.

In the middle of this silence.

In the middle of my uncertainty.

In the middle of all the rational reasons I had to doubt, disbelieve, and walk away from God.

I had to make a choice.

Would I choose to believe in a God I could no longer feel, understand, hear, make sense of, or, in many ways, even remember? Or would I choose to make this decision based on the same thing I'd based every other decision I ever made in my life on: *my feelings?*

Would I choose to believe my *feelings* of God not being real and my *feelings* of doubt? Or would I choose to put my faith in the God I had committed my life to, the God I believed saved me from suicide?

Our Choices Define Us

I remembered a scene from a book I'd read years ago when I first met God. It was a book about the importance and power of faith. The author, Lee Strobel, tells the story of Charles Templeton, a close friend of the great evangelist Billy Graham. Both Templeton and Graham worked as evangelists, speaking in arenas to tens of thousands of people about faith in Jesus Christ.

But eventually, Templeton began to doubt. He and Graham had deep discussions over things like the reliability of the Bible. But Graham held on to his faith, and despite the challenges to accept things like the biblical account of creation, he would choose to believe the Bible was God's Word.

"I believe the Genesis account of creation because it's in the Bible," said Graham. "I've discovered something in my ministry: When I take the Bible literally, when I proclaim it as the Word of God, my preaching has *power*. When I stand on the platform and say, 'God says,' or 'The Bible says,' the Holy Spirit uses me. There are results. Wiser men than you or I have been arguing questions like this for centuries. I don't have the time or the intellect to examine all sides of the theological dispute, so I've decided once for all to stop questioning and accept the Bible as God's Word."

"But Billy, you cannot do that," replied Templeton. "You don't dare stop thinking about the most important question in life. Do it and you begin to die. It's intellectual suicide."

"I don't know about anybody else," Graham said, "but I've decided that that's the path for me."

About fifty years later, Strobel interviewed Templeton for his book. Templeton said that he still didn't believe in God or the Bible. Strobel asked, "What do you think about Jesus at this stage of your life?" The question revealed a softness in Templeton.

"[Jesus] was the greatest human being who has ever lived. He was a moral genius. His ethical sense was unique. He was intrinsically the wisest person that I've ever encountered in my life or in my readings. His commitment was total and led to his own death, much to the detriment of the world. What could one say about him except that this was a form of greatness?"

Strobel was shocked. "You sound like you really care about him."

"Well, yes, he is the most important thing in my life," said Templeton. "I . . . I . . . I . . . I know it may sound strange, but I have to say . . . I adore him." Templeton sounded like he genuinely loved Jesus.

Then, Templeton uttered the words Strobel never expected to hear from him. "And if I may put it this way, I . . . miss . . . him!" Emotion overwhelmed him and he wept. After a few moments, he composed himself, then dismissively said, "Enough of that."[1] I related to Templeton's words in this scene. I missed Jesus so deeply as I questioned the reality of God.

In many ways, I had unconsciously rejected the Holy Spirit of God in my deception. I followed this love affair, thinking God had "called" me to help this poor suicidal man whom no one understood. I had deceived myself into thinking I could be the savior that this wounded person had tried to turn me into. I rejected what people who loved me and loved God had to say.

I trusted in my feelings rather than pursuing the context and heart of the Bible that had been so alive and faithful to guide me for so many years. I trusted in my short-sighted reasoning rather than pursuing the Holy Spirit for deeper revelation than the surface level one I'd interpreted about a dream in such a perverted way. I didn't realize that God meant for me to pursue him deeper in the questionable times, and that he was never afraid of my questions.

You will seek me and find me when you seek me with all your heart.[2]

The more I clung to my own understanding above trusting God, the more I had unconsciously rejected him. By this time I'd trained my ears to ignore God's voice even when he did speak.

And so I sat alone with this choice I had to make.

No person.

No Scripture.

No God I could hear or sense.

Would I love God and put my faith in him like I said I would always do so long ago, in many moments of deep worship and prayer? Or would I now consciously reject him?

I didn't *feel* him. Because of this, I wasn't sure I believed in him anymore. It came down a choice. I had to just choose.

So I did.

Beyond Emotions

Wiping my tears, I told my emotions to be quiet. I couldn't talk clearly enough with all the sobbing. I needed to make a confession. I needed to speak out my decision so my ears and all of heaven and hell could hear me.

"I'm going to choose *you*. I'm going to choose to believe and not doubt," I said aloud.

I chose against my own mind and soul.

I chose to believe.

I chose to put my faith in God, the way someone who may be questioning their love for their spouse chooses to go on with a marriage. I would continue. I would commit. I would move on and trust, no matter if he never spoke to me again. I would surrender. And if love was a choice, it was in this moment I chose to love.

"But God," I spoke again, risking the weight of his silence. "How will I ever get up from this floor and not think of this person that I have to let go of in order to live and love you? He is everywhere. I don't know how I will make it out of this."

Shhhhhh . . .

I felt God press on my heart with the weight of his love for the first time in what felt like forever. The pain of it was almost unbearable. I crumpled to the ground weeping as I felt him speaking to my heart.

Aren't I the light? Aren't I the one that gives you eyes to see and a mind to understand? Didn't I give you a heart to delight in my mysteries hidden for you to seek out and find? I delight in you exploring the mysteries I have hidden for you. Aren't I the one who calls the sun to come up and paints the sky in different colors? Isn't the rainbow my promise? Isn't it true that your heart burns when you come close to me? It wasn't ever him you were longing for when you thought you were in love with him. It was always me.

I cried as he went on bringing revelation.

Think of me when you see rainbows in water. Think of my throne of grace where I invite you to come and be with me as my friend and my bride. Think of me when you remember true love and sacrificing one life for another. Think of me when you wake up, and when it gets quiet and all you can hear is the breath I've given you. The burning in your heart was always over me. And the burning in his was always for me as well. I am the one who gives you life and has made it beautiful. Enjoy it, and when you do, remember me and how extravagantly I love you. Remember me, Lacey, my beloved, and you will live.

I fell asleep right there on the floor and didn't wake until the sun was setting. It was the deepest sleep I'd had in a year. The weight was lifted and the nausea was gone. I was hungry in my body but even more so in my spirit.

Hero Note:
Joelene Sturm

Meet Joelene Sturm, who happens to be my sister-in-law. She is a hero to me in many ways. She fights the lies of discouragement with a powerful gift of encouragement. She has been through seasons of silence from God and I have seen her come through with the most beautifully committed heart to her Savior in ways that make me want to love God deeper.

Here is a letter to you, from Joelene.

Dear Reader,

Nobody is too far away from God's love. If you ever choose to walk away from him, I believe you would be walking away from the greatest adventure that God has for your life. The truth is no matter how far we run, our Father is right behind us with open arms just waiting for us to turn around.

If I could go back to age nineteen, I would tell myself not to look to others for my worth. I would tell myself that I am a cherished treasure and that I deserve to be treated and loved as such. And so I am telling you now, you are a precious, treasured child of the King and are dearly loved by your heavenly Father.

In his love,
Joelene Sturm
wife, mom, musician, songwriter

Reach for me and I'll never let you go. I'll never leave you now. Reach for me. My arms are waiting for you to reach for me.

Joelene Sturm, "Reach for Me"

13

THE MYSTERY OF
Renewal

All Scripture is inspired by God and is useful to teach
us what is true and to make us realize what is wrong
in our lives. It corrects us when we are wrong and
teaches us to do what is right. God uses it to prepare
and equip his people to do every good work.

2 Timothy 3:16–17 NLT

*W*hen I came to my senses, there were no physical arms
to fall into. For the longest time I had pushed away
all of the wisest and most loving voices in my life. Now, there was
no one standing beneath me, waiting with open arms, on the day I
fell violently away from the lies I had believed about love. My faith
in Christ had been based on what I felt in my heart. But my life
could no longer be built on my deceptive heart and fickle feelings
that had almost killed me.

I felt fragile. Shaken. Small. Breakable. Unsafe with myself. Life
itself felt fragile. I realized life was a gift from God, and I had been

trying to live mine by making God into whatever I wanted him to be in the moment, whatever felt good to me at the time.

I have tears in my eyes as I write this because I realize this is what my orphan heart was like. I'd run ahead thinking I had to make it on my own, even with voices all around me yelling "Stop!" I wouldn't trust any voice more than my own feelings and reasoning. I had lumped them into the same suspicious category as all the abusive authority I had seen in my lifetime. Orphan wisdom had made me my own final, rebellious authority.

It's only after I had run ahead into the street, ignoring all the warnings, that the eighteen-wheeler came zooming by with a force that should have sucked me under its tires. Instead it threw me off the road with the loudness of danger still ringing in my ears. That's where I was now—picking myself up off the side of the road after a brush with death, realizing I was safe. Fear of God and a revelation of the fragility of life washed over me like an electric shock, pulsing through my heart in waves.

This feeling reminded me of the first time I almost wrecked my car. I was wearing sandals and one slipped off. I tried to slip it back on and accidently jerked the wheel into oncoming traffic. When I tried to correct it, I almost ran into the guardrail on the other side. The oncoming traffic was stopping, but when I pushed the brake my shoe was in the way. I pressed the shoe down, thinking it would engage the brake, but it was sitting at an angle and hit the accelerator instead. Just as I was about to slam into the car in front of me, the shoe slipped free and I punched the brake.

I pulled over as soon as I could, trembling. I cried for a minute as I tried to gather myself, thanking God I wasn't dead. Then I called a friend to pick me up. I didn't want to drive anymore.

Deciding to Let the Bible Drive

That's how I felt when I woke up that evening.

I didn't want to drive anymore.

I had no one to hold me, no one to cry with me, no one to rejoice with me over the fact that I hadn't been destroyed in the mess I made. I was tempted to ask God to speak to me again. But I was also scared to. I was nervous because I had such a deep fear of God that I didn't want to hear him wrong again. I didn't want to assume I had the right to approach God after I had run away from him so defiantly.

So I did the only thing I knew to do.

I decided to put my faith in the Bible again.

I went to a Christian bookstore to get a new Bible. I stood there staring at the rows of Bibles, searching for a title that sounded familiar. When I saw the *Life Application Study Bible* I remembered this was the one a friend had told me about. She loved it. I tucked it under my arm along with *The Quest Bible* I'd already found and was squeezing tightly to my chest. If I could have shoved those Bibles directly into my heart, I would have. I held on to them like they were the only things keeping me alive. After swiping my debit card, I calculated that I had less than ten dollars left in my bank account. This was it. I wasn't sure where my next meal was coming from, but I knew I needed the Scripture's refuge and nourishment for my soul more than anything else.

Diving back into the Bible was a choice. I chose to keep believing that God had written these words. Even though, in my deception, I had taken it all out of context, perverted its meaning to say what I wanted it to say. Even though, to my own detriment, I had taken some parts and rejected other parts. I never wanted to say, "I feel like God is speaking this to me," because it was this *feeling* that had led to all my deception. Instead I would go straight to the Scriptures.

I studied different subjects using the concordances. Subjects like deception, false prophets, silence from God, hearing God wrong, adultery, coveting, and repentance.

It wasn't easy. I was starting over in many ways. I dove into his Word like it was all that mattered. Because to me, it was.

They made fun of me at work because all I did was read the Bible on my breaks. I wasn't interested in having friends or being nice to people. I didn't trust myself or anyone else. I was locking up my heart in a protective way. I think during the healing process it is natural to be shut off and overly cautious. But when you break your leg and years later you're still wearing your cast, you may need rehabilitation to help you understand you've healed and that it's possible to walk without the confines that were necessary during the healing process. I didn't understand that.

I remember reading a book called *The Four Loves* by C. S. Lewis. One quote, in particular, kept repeating in my head long after I read it.

> To love at all is to be vulnerable. Love anything and your heart will be wrung and possibly broken. If you want to make sure of keeping it intact, you must give it to no one, not even an animal. Wrap it carefully round with hobbies and little luxuries; avoid all entanglements. Lock it up safe in the casket or coffin of your selfishness. But in that casket safe, dark, motionless, airless, it will change. It will not be broken; it will become unbreakable, impenetrable, and irredeemable. To love is to be vulnerable.[1]

I realized this was the path I was on. But Lewis's words told me how wrong it was to isolate my heart forever. It was like I was sitting alone in my house with the doors locked, reading about how to love my neighbor, and when my neighbor knocked on my door I'd yell out, "Go away, leave me alone! I'm learning how to love people in here."

I had begun to grow cold toward others. I doubted my ability to show the hope I had found to those who needed it. I was like the prodigal son. When he returned to his father after hitting bottom, he pleaded with him to be treated like one of his father's servants. That was his mentality. Just make me a servant. But his father would have none of that. He restored him to his status as son and heir.

Even though I had returned to God, I was stuck in the unhealthy mindset that I was not worthy to be his daughter. But God will have none of that.

Hero Note:

Robb Kelley

Meet Robb Kelley. He is a hero to me because
of his reckless surrender to all that God would
ask him to do. He is a missionary to all those
around him, pouring out his life and heart for
the purpose of bringing God's love, light, glory, and
revelation to the earth. His impact on me saved my life,
and confirmed my calling in music as well. He is a spiritual father in many
ways, and I'm so thankful for his influence in my life.

Here is a note to you, from Robb.

Dear Reader,

Make the pursuit of Jesus and the knowledge of who he
really is the magnum opus (greatest work) of your life.
Do not just encounter him as your Savior. Press on to
know him as Father, Friend, Healer, Deliverer, Counselor,
Confidant, and all he wants to be for you. From the
endless treasure of his genuine identity, know his perfect
love. Then from whatever you receive experientially from
his divine nature, go forth and give that away. The
world desperately cries out for what you possess of
him.

Miracles will follow your sharing of Christ! The
impossible is possible with God leading the way. Seek,
hear, and obey him. Watch what he does! Along the way,
never give up. Serve and love well those you are blessed to
come in contact with. It's an epic journey and battle

we are born into. With Christ in us and leading us, we can and will fulfill our divine destiny.

Love,

Robb Kelley
husband, writer, speaker, pastor

Sometimes we can pass around the phrase "against all odds" like free samples of our favorite coffee. But in reality those types of crossroad moments, either clinging to Christ or to our own faulty understanding, end up fully defining our lives and the legacy we leave in the earth.

Robb Kelley, "Knocked Down but Not Out"

14

THE MYSTERY OF
Choosing to Be a Daughter

> Honor your father and your mother. Then you will live a long, full life in the land the LORD your God is giving you.
>
> Exodus 20:12 NLT

> [Jesus] replied to him, "Who is my mother and who are my brothers? . . . For whoever does the will of my Father in heaven is my brother and sister and mother."
>
> Matthew 12:48–50

*I*t was the sound of running water. The faint clinking of dishes being washed. That was what woke me. I opened my eyes to see the ceiling a foot above my face. I didn't recognize the bed I was in. As I lay there, trying to remember where I was, I began to hear an angelic voice singing in the distance.

"I adore you," she sang. "I will sing it with all my heart . . . I adore you . . . I love everything you are."

It was Sarah. I was so tired the night before that I had slept in my work clothes. I didn't remember falling asleep. I had driven two hours after work, from Temple to Dallas, to come up here and be with Eric and Sarah for a couple days.

I thought of the conversation I had with Eric.

"We'd love to see you, Lace," he had said.

"Well it's kinda far to drive after work. But it would be good to see y'all too," I said, considering his invitation.

"Sarah says she can make up the top bunk of the kids' bed for you, and you can sleep in as late as you want. But of course it's up to you."

I wondered about his words: "We'd love to see you."

I wondered how much truth was in them. I hadn't talked to them in so long. My last conversation with Eric had ended so terribly. I couldn't imagine what he thought of me after everything. He knew about the affair before I even realized what was happening. He had tried to warn me. But I didn't listen. He never showed me that he was upset or angry at me for how I responded so hatefully, but I still wondered.

My Pendulum Heart

As I lay in the bed that morning, listening to Sarah sing to Jesus while she washed dishes, I felt a deep sense of welcome that brought a peace to my heart and made me cry. It's funny how I could sense the truth of someone's heart toward me one minute then question it the next. That was how my orphan heart related to people: extreme trust, then

unreasonable distrust. Letting them use my toothbrush one moment and not even able to speak to them the next. "I need you to save me!" in the same breath as "I don't need anyone; I can save myself!" My heart was a swinging pendulum.

I got up, walked out of the room, and asked Sarah to remind me where the bathroom was. She didn't hear me at first and kept washing dishes. A wave of doubt swept over me. Why was I here again?

Look how busy she is. You're just a pity project for them. They don't have time to deal with your questions, a voice whispered.

I saw a small batch of eggs on the counter beside her.

And she feels like she has to feed you. They can't afford to feed you. You should get out of here.

My orphan heart was taunting me.

I prayed for God to bless Sarah as she sang. I prayed that I wouldn't be a burden or a distraction to her and Eric while I was there. I prayed I could help out somehow. So I cleared my throat and talked louder this time.

"Good morning, Sarah."

She looked up, turned around, and smiled broad and bright.

"Hi, Lace!" Her voice was full of joy and peace. "How did you sleep?"

"Honestly, Sarah, I slept so well. I forgot where I was." I laughed.

"Oh, good!" She smiled.

"There is so much peace here. It's just so peaceful. Thanks for letting me stay here. Is there anything I can help with?" I wondered sheepishly, feeling guilty again for imposing.

"Oh, no, Lace, we love to have you here. I made some eggs for you, right there on the counter."

My brain accused me again, *See, she thinks she has to feed you. She has three kids! Don't eat her food. She needs it for her kids.*

I stood there feeling guilty that she had made me food. All of the sudden, I remembered a Scripture: "If you enter a town and they welcome you, eat whatever is set before you."

"Thank you," I told her finally, and took the eggs. As I sat eating, I wondered about their schedule and whether it would be inconvenient for them if I were to take a shower now. I wasn't sure what time it was.

"I put a towel on the chair for you if you want to shower. The bathroom is the middle door in the hallway, in case you forgot."

I was relieved she brought it up first.

Trusting God While Waiting for the Loving Cut

The rest of the day, I read my Bible and wrote in my journal like usual. After the kids had gone to bed, Sarah made coffee. She, Eric, and I sat on their fluffy couches and sipped from our hot mugs.

"It's so great to have you with us," Eric said.

But I had such a hard time believing him. In my mind I battled. I heard, *Lacey, they're trying really hard to make you feel welcome because they feel like they have to fix you. You're their pity project.*

It was my orphan response to their kindness. I tried to ignore it while we talked. Sarah daintily held her coffee cup and listened with a furrowed brow. I was uncomfortably spilling my guts about the painful past two months. Without averting her sparkling, blue, squinted eyes, she pulled her feet up into her chair and tucked them underneath her, the way short people do. Even in this movement she held good posture. I don't know why this bothered me. Her mouth was small and her voice was quiet, but her words were sharp. She had a way of cutting you in the places you loved most, like a surgeon going right to the source, but you're conscious and you just want to scream, "Leave in my malignant tumor! I don't want you to cut me!"

They were mostly busy with their kids, their house, and their family's needs—and now they were so graciously busy with me. I felt lucky that I got this moment with them, and also nervous and on edge. I knew Sarah was going to cut me when I finished talking.

Why was I sitting here? Because I was certain God wanted me to. Did I feel honestly invited, or loved by them? Not really. They said they loved me, but I never understood what that meant to them. They always said that it was a "pleasure" to help me, but I could never believe that they were ever pleased to be around me. Probably because they had priorities, boundaries, and order in their life that made me feel uncomfortable because I couldn't understand them.

I trusted that God was doing something in these moments with Sarah and Eric that was changing me for the better. And although I didn't get them, I knew I needed to listen. They were the voice of God, and this voice was ugly at times and hard to listen to, and it made me want to break things and run screaming from the room. But if I could look past the voice and honor the message, I would find wisdom that pushed me into a peace I had never been in before.

Sarah the Gentle Exorcist

Sarah is extraordinary in the way she helps people get rid of their demons.

Have you ever seen one of those creepy videos of a preacher casting a demon out of someone with his booming voice, sweating, shaking, and using King James English? I don't know exactly what I think about those videos. I do know that there have been strongholds in my way of thinking that were demonic—ways of thinking that needed to be exorcised like a preacher might exorcise a demon out of someone. Without deliverance from these thought patterns, I could never be free and fully live the way God intended.

Sarah has a gift of deliverance. But she doesn't yell, sweat, or speak in Latin whenever she is bringing deliverance to someone.

She simply makes gentle, quiet statements of blessing and love. Deliverance for me was a process. Repentance means to change the way you think. When you try and change old patterns of thinking, either you weep with revelation or you rage with offense and collapse in emptiness where the stronghold made a hole in your soul as it left with a scream. Like me.

Sarah smiled at me with a victory sigh when I was done talking. "You sound like you are healthier than ever," she said.

What? Healthy? What does that mean? I felt my face get hot, the heat spreading down my arms and tingling my fingers. I felt like my soul was trembling with anger at her words. I sat still while my mind raced with uncertainty. *Does that mean I'm becoming the kind of boring, passionless, emotionless, suburban, selfish, fearful, fake girl I always feel sorry for? Is this what* healthy *is to this lady? Does that mean I've lost who I am? Who does she think I'm supposed to be, anyway?*

What's Deeper Than Sickness?

All of these thoughts exposed a destructive spiritual stronghold in my life. The very way I thought about "being healthy" exposed a false sense of identity. I'd learned it from Tim Burton movies, from metal music, from dark poetry and art. I reveled in honesty and brokenness and loved to celebrate strange ideas and ways of life. I loved the rebellion of being different and the isolation that came from feeling superior because I seemed to see life in a different color than everyone else.

This sense of being *different* was my fuel for wanting to create art. I wanted to sing a song no one was singing. I wanted to shock people with a different way of living and seeing things. But in doing this I had judged all the "healthy" people as the enemies of art and change and beauty. I didn't want peace. I wanted struggle, chaos. I wanted to embrace the sickness of life. This was *truth*. To think anything else would be naïve, shallow, and dead! I thought it was "deep" to stay in the mess. But the health Sarah was referring to was not the shallow naïveté of ignorance and denial I thought it was. In society, at times, it feels like it's "deeper" to recognize society's bluff of what it calls happiness than to pretend nothing is wrong.

But there is a depth beyond acknowledging what's wrong. It's called "becoming healthy." And this is what Sarah was calling me to.

She was not asking me to become a shallow faker. She was asking me to let go of wallowing in the sickness, to venture beyond it and embrace healing. But when she suggested I heal, the part in me that wanted to revel in my sickness was bothered.

At the time, I couldn't understand why her calling me *healthy* made me so livid. A few months prior, I might have screamed. Proverbs says, "Fools vent their anger, but the wise quietly hold it back" (29:11 NLT). *Hold back.* I had been foolish in many ways over the past few years, and this was one of them. I wasn't one to think about what I felt. I was one to feel and express *as* I felt. Immediately. And then, generally, I regretted it because my brash expression produced the opposite of what I would have hoped for.

How to Choose to Become a Daughter

But.

I began to analyze my thoughts and feelings.

Love is not a feeling. It is a choice. I remembered a Bible verse I read recently—the one that kept coming up everywhere I went: "God sets the lonely in families" (Ps. 68:6). I realized I had a choice to make in that moment. Would I tell my feelings to shut up and trust that God had blessed me with Eric and Sarah as safe voices in my life?

I thought of what Eric originally proposed: "God wants to remove your orphan identity." But it was up to me. I had to *choose.*

Did I want to be their daughter? Would I soften my heart and listen, even when I didn't want to? Would I trust the safety in their advice and encouragement, even if I was inclined to doubt? Would I submit to their words even when the words made me feel angry at times? I had to try. It was so clear that I had to make a choice whether to soften my heart or run.

I chose to soften. I decided to listen.

I began to ask myself, *Is this the right way to feel? Is this going to make sense to you, or anyone else, when you start yelling whatever comes out of this anger?* I sat still and analyzed, waiting. I was quiet. Sadness descended on me in that moment like a five-foot blanket of snow.

This is what it feels like when someone tells you that everything you knew about love is twisted and wrong, and you hate them for it but you know they are right. Your entire soul wants to bully your mind, mouth, and body into rebellion against their words. You want to make cases against the prophet herself—in this case, Sarah. You want to tell her why she's perverted. You want to run away. You want to claim that you are being victimized and abused by her speaking this truth. And your soul flings hatred at her.

Why? Because your perverted soul hates the truth.

The reason for the hatred is because you are completely addicted to the twisted love that has flooded your body with adrenaline for so long. How could you ever live without it? How could anyone suggest that? What does *she* know? She's not going to control you! Your soul is stomping around and growling like a monster.

But your mind, your spirit—they begin to speak. Whispering behind the soul's back.

She has no agenda. She just wants to help you. She's tired. She's not getting paid for this. She has to get up in three hours to feed her infant child and yet she has chosen to sit with you. She has no reason to want to control you.

She loves you. That's why she's here. She loves you enough to tell you the truth. Even if you might hate her for it. She is even saying it kindly, like love does. She is not attacking you. She is loving you. Be still. Listen. Tell your soul to be still. Tell your soul to receive. Because your soul will kill you if you don't control it.

Whoever "I" was, in that moment, became still. The monster inside grew smaller, still screaming, but sounding more and more like a shrinking devil. By the time Sarah came over to sit with me on my chair, put her arm around me, and tuck her head on my rigid shoulder, the monster sounded like a squeaky little mouse. The Bible says if we resist the enemy then he will flee from us. But I wasn't used to resisting this way. It was exhausting. I felt like burying my exhausted heart in a hole in the ground. Maybe it would feel warmer in a grave than under the five feet of snowy nothingness I felt right then, covering me from head to toe.

I felt empty, yet heavy. I just wanted to sleep. Someone once told me sleep is the brother of death. I think that's why I was longing for it.

Hero Note:

Sarah Patrick

Meet Sarah Patrick. She is a hero to me because she has great faith. She is willing to pour out her life every moment in order to be obedient to her heavenly Father because she knows he loves her. She taught me that *his way is the best way!* She also taught me that God is our defense when we can't defend ourselves.

Here is a note to you, from Sarah.

Dear Reader,

God is love. He is love inside and out, and you cannot be torn, removed, hidden, or snatched from his love. Too often, those who have been hurt or decimated by life begin to believe God is a broken lover too. But he isn't. He is and forever will be Love. He is and forever will be loving you.

I often think of myself in my early teenage years and how wild and big and full of possibility the world looked. How there was a whisper in my heart that said I was made to be wild and full of possibility too. Too often I let fear, doubt, and other voices convince me I was mistaken—I wasn't really called, chosen, or wanted. But I was wrong. Those whispers were invitations from God.

I would love to go back and tell myself, "Don't ever be afraid of saying yes to an invitation from God. Be bolder than you think normal, dream bigger than you think wise, and say yes to every invitation from God. Even when you are afraid, say yes."

With the Father's love,

Sarah K. Patrick

wife, mom, blogger/writer, photographer

God is not interested in having slaves he uses and then discards. He is interested in an eternal beautiful friendship with you—the real and honest you.

Sarah K. Patrick[1]

I learned
many things
about how to
view my heart
as a treasure
worth protecting.

15

THE MYSTERY OF
Many Crowns

Now that you have purified yourselves by obeying the truth so that you have sincere love for each other, love one another deeply, from the heart.

1 Peter 1:22

I was twenty-three when I finally chose to become a daughter. By the time I was twenty-six, I had learned the concepts of honor, submission, and obedience. I once thought submission and obedience were only appropriate for dogs. I thought, *What? Submit? Obey? Are you a fascist? Where is the exit?* But Eric and Sarah never even hinted at telling me what to do. There was no manipulation, no guilt-tripping, no trying to change my *no* to a *yes*, not even a sales pitch to get me to go the way they thought I should. They only loved me by *honoring my freedom.*

They asked me questions so I could come to my own conclusions. They gave me suggestions when I wanted advice. But they always made sure I knew I needed to make my own choices. Within this safe and loving relationship I built with Eric and Sarah, my willing submission and obedience to their wisdom actually brought me freedom, safety, peace, and joy. I realized during this time I wasn't merely submitting to two ordinary, flawed people. *I was submitting to how God was teaching me what it means to be a daughter.* I was trusting God to protect me as I submitted, and he always did.

When I honored Eric and Sarah's words, I saw miraculous safety, health, and wholeness unfold in every direction of my life. All my judgments began to crumble and I learned many things about how to view my heart as a treasure worth protecting. I learned that wearing the crown of a daughter is actually many crowns in one.

In the film *The Eternal Sunshine of a Spotless Mind*, lead character Clementine is not just an open book to everyone she meets, she's a Niagara Falls of a person, with no reservations—a cataract of being. When Clementine meets Joel, the other lead character, he is eating lunch. He's struck by how she introduces herself and then immediately takes a piece of his chicken. She asks, of course, but never waits for an answer. She just takes it. Joel is stunned by her ability to be immediately intimate, "Like we were already lovers," he says. She reminds me so much of my younger self.

I realize now, when I think of her character, that the tumultuous life she lived and the sort of the death wish she carried were the result of the way she was so reckless with her heart. She was open to immediate emotional intimacy with anyone, and it turned out to be destructive to her heart and the hearts of her lovers.

How much of me do I let out? All of me, all the time, to all people? I used to think the artistic, free answer was *yes*. But as I become emotionally healthy, I realized that the deeper and wiser answer is *no*. There's a special beauty to remaining hidden to most, revealed to some. This type of beauty is powerful. The ability to reserve your heart, out of love for yourself and honor for the God who made you, makes your display of certain parts of your heart sacred and precious. The gift of your friendship, romance, or child's or parent's heart becomes so much more valuable to the one you choose to give it to. Slowly, I was learning this.

When I visit my niece in her home, she's free to run around in her own house, with her family, in her PJs—or underwear!—and it's okay. But, when her mom says, "Okay Sammy-girl, we're going out to eat," she puts on her favorite twirly dress. It's not fakery. She can enjoy being the side of herself that sports her favorite twirly dress and relate to the general public in honorable, beautiful ways while wearing appropriate clothing for a restaurant. Different clothes for different occasions equals a different way to act while remaining true to who you are. For me, it feels like picking a crown to wear that reminds me how to relate to each situation. I'm not playing dress up. I'm just sharing the part of me that makes the most sense for the circumstances.

There are moments within my most intimate relationships, like with my closest friends or my sisters, where we may feel free to go without a crown at all, nothing hidden or held back. But *even in these relationships* there are moments where, for the sake of love or circumstance, we put on our crowns to honor one another. I used to think that saying whatever you think, whenever you think it, was being honest and intimate and that it's just what friends did. I now realize that if they are hurtful, out of place, or discouraging, those words are often really just selfish venting and are not rooted in real love.

There are also moments when I can sense that the wise thing to do is to remove myself from a situation. If a married man starts speaking to me in a romantic way, he is no longer relating to me as a friend or someone whom I should help. He is now relating to me as an enemy. Does the Bible say to love our enemies? Yes. But I can love him by "fleeing sexual immorality" as the Bible also says. Running away from someone who is toying with the idea of being spiritually, relationally, or emotionally destructive is the most loving thing I can do for both of us. "Fleeing" is also important when I feel myself beginning to connect deeply in an emotional way with someone who is off-limits. Running away in those moments can feel awkward and rude. But in the end, it is better to be thought rude than to have to sort through the risk of either of you developing "in love" feelings that won't lead anywhere good.

There are lots of great books out there about how we fall in and out of love, and most of them are marriage books. I wish someone would have talked about those things to me when I was single. It helps me to stay faithful in my marriage, but the truth is that if I really wanted my heart to honor marriage, I should have trained my heart to have self-control, flee sexual immorality, and stay faithful before marriage.

This is how I started to understand which "crown" to wear for the appropriate relationship or situation. Identifying the different categories a relationship falls into has helped me create healthy boundaries for my relationships. And within those boundaries, I found freedom. Here are the categories I identified:

mothers and fathers
brothers and sisters
friends
daughters and sons
acquaintances/strangers
enemies

Mothers and Fathers

I relate to mothers and fathers with a particular respect. These people are generally older than me. They are people I want to learn from. I can see the fruit of love, wisdom, and righteousness in their lives that I want to develop in my own life.

They are safe places. I can express an open, soft-hearted, childlike receptiveness toward them. This safety, then, allows me to submit to their guidance even in things I don't always understand. I take their suggestions seriously. I honor, respect, and bless them in special ways.

Brothers and Sisters

Brothers and sisters are people who share the same faith and values I do. I honor them in similar ways as a mother or father, but don't take their words so personally.

I look for ways to serve and encourage them.

Friends

Friends are generally brothers and sisters who sharpen me and allow me to sharpen them, meaning I can be vulnerable about my struggles. We can admit we don't have all the answers and listen to each other's hearts. As we do this, we learn and grow from each other.

We are open and honest in a way that we aren't with everyone. We walk side by side with one another and experience life together: joy, pain, growth, trials, and changes.

Daughters and Sons

Daughters and sons are gifts. They will often watch me to see how to live. God gives me a deep unconditional love for them.

I intentionally set out to teach them and provide wisdom for them. I'm protective toward them. I'll correct them if they are willing to receive it, always with kind gentleness. *But only when they have invited me to speak into a certain area of their lives.* I'm always reminding myself that God loves them more than I do and that ultimately, they belong to him. Also, we must choose each other. If I feel motherly toward someone who doesn't view me as a mother, then I can't relate to them with a mother's heart or they will just run from me and tell everyone how smothering I am. If someone looks up to me as a mom but I don't feel peace about taking on that role, for whatever reason, then I need to be clear with them about that. Many times I've seen this lead them to another mentor relationship that is better for whatever reason.

Having a spiritual mentoring relationship is an amazing gift from God, but I believe, like natural parenting, it only lasts to certain degrees, for the season that God has called it to last.

Acquaintances/Strangers

Acquaintances and strangers are people who may not share my values, faith, or mission. In fact, they may hold values that contradict mine. Their beliefs may seem to undermine my faith and what I feel I'm called to do and become and believe.

They are people whom God loves. Jesus has died for them. They are to be honored as *creations* of my Lord. But I don't consider their opinions or comments in the same way I do those of my friends or family.

Enemies

Enemies are people who don't share my values. They may actively try to hurt me emotionally, spiritually, or physically. They desire harmful things for me.

Or, they may not purposely harm me, but they do it consistently. I seek to *bless and love them,* in any way possible, *so long as it doesn't enable them to hurt me or themselves.*

Knowing which relationships I'm called to and which ones I'm not is important. I don't always have enough space in my life to connect with everyone I want to. It's kind of like a LEGO piece; I only have so many available connection points. That's why it's important to know which relationships I'm called to focus on for each season. Even Jesus only had twelve people he poured into on a regular basis, and out of those twelve, three with whom he was closest. If Jesus could only have twelve, what does that say about my capacity?

I watched Eric and Sarah as they dealt with different people. Sarah talked to her older daughter much differently than she talked to her younger daughter. Eric talked to me much differently than he spoke to the guys in my band. They dealt with me genuinely and intentionally with kindness, but they never compromised their relationships with their children or each other to minister to me. That's because they have healthy priorities and boundaries.

During this time, when God called me to honor them as my spiritual parents, he covered their actions with grace. All along, God blessed my desire to honor Eric as a spiritual authority in my life, and at the same time he would never allow me to turn Eric and Sarah into idols or gods. Whenever I would start to put them in the wrong place in my heart, God showed me their humanity. Sometimes they needed my forgiveness, and I was thankful to know that.

16

THE MYSTERY OF
Loving an Idea
versus Loving a Person

After this many of his disciples turned back and no
longer walked with him. So Jesus said to the Twelve,
"Do you want to go away as well?" Simon Peter answered him, "Lord, to whom shall we go? You have the
words of eternal life, and we have believed, and have
come to know, that you are the Holy One of God."

John 6:66–69 ESV

The more I learned to cultivate self-control in my emotions,
the more I felt free to submit to Eric and Sarah as mentors.
They never demanded I do anything. I don't think they ever
even *asked* me to do anything. They only shared how they felt

and gently shared their views on whatever we were discussing. It was always up to me whether I honored what they had to say. They never seemed to expect me to do that either. There was no pressure or manipulative disappointment if I didn't go with their opinion.

Little by little, I could tell that being a daughter meant to submit to my parents and to honor them as best as I could in everything. One of the things that made Eric and Sarah feel safe was watching them pray, worship, and discuss the Scriptures. They weren't just making things up as they went along. They submitted to God's leading through his Holy Spirit, his order in the home, their spiritual family, and ultimately the Scriptures. They daily sought to hear from the Lord about how to handle each situation.

Speaking truth in love, we will in all things grow up.[1]

There comes a time to grow up.

I remember how in fifth and sixth grade my classmates started to gauge maturity by "how far you had gone" with someone. Kissing was a big deal. Romance and sexuality was supposed to be the mark of maturity. But I realize now how debasing that is. It reduces the way we talk about human maturity to the same way we talk about animal maturity. Self-fulfillment rather than self-control defines us, and this leads to destruction in our relationships and in our mental and spiritual lives.

Eric and Sarah taught me the importance of keeping my heart pure before the Lord. This cultivated self-control. I quickly learned that self-discipline was the first step toward maturity.

As children, we pitch fits when we don't get what we want. Was I now, as an adult, still throwing selfish tantrums? Again, I needed to make a choice: to continue to pitch my grown-up fits or to live self-controlled. Perhaps our fits are simply more socially acceptable, grown-up forms of the same kind of childish manipulation?

Manipulation or Maturity?

Manipulation is embedded in our DNA. It comes from fear. It comes from wanting to control things so they will go our way. We're afraid if we don't manipulate to get things to go our way we will miss out, or things won't go well for us or others. A manipulative spirit, I've learned, stems from an untrusting spirit. As a mom, I'm trying to teach my toddlers to trust that I have good in mind for them.

One day my son was having a meltdown because he wasn't allowed to eat candy before he ate his lunch. When the meltdown occurred, I no longer needed to address the issue of the candy. I needed to address the fit. So I told him a story.

"Once upon a time, there were two little boys. A big brother and a little brother. It was about time for lunch and the big brother noticed a container full of tiny, colorful chocolate candies. 'Mom, can I have some of these chocolate candies?' said the big brother.

"But before his momma could answer, the little brother ran into the kitchen, 'I want chocolate candies! I want chocolate candies! Can I have some too?'

"The mother said, 'You are not allowed to have any candies right now. You must eat some lunch first.'

"The little brother fell to the ground kicking and screaming. 'I want candies. I want candies!'

"The mother picked up the little one and put him in time-out. She came back to the quiet kitchen, and the big brother was standing there beside the candies.

"'Son, you are not allowed to have them now either.'

"The older brother had learned what to say to his mother's no.

"'Okay, Mom. I know you love me.'

"Whenever he said this to his mother, he was planting a seed in his mother's heart to let her know he trusted her. He knew that the words, 'Okay, Mom, I know you love me' were a seed of trust that carried a blessing inside it. It blessed his mother for him to trust her and filled her heart with joy and peace. And because her heart was filled with joy and peace, she began to think of ways she could bless the boy and reward him for his precious gift of trust.

"*Buzz*! The timer rang. Time-out was over for the younger brother. So she let him know his time was done. He ran right into the kitchen. 'Can I have the candies now?'

"'No my son,' she said again. But by this time she had pulled a cake out of the oven. Before the boy saw the cake, he fell to the floor crying and pitching another fit. She took him back to his room. When the timer rang again, she told the little brother he could come out and by this time she was about to frost the cake.

"'Now can I have the candies?'

"'No. Don't ask me for the candies again or you will go into time-out *again*.'

"So, again, the younger boy fell to the ground and pitched a fit. By this time, the older brother was playing outside while his mom finished making lunch. The mother sent the younger son to time-out, and he cried so long she thought he might never come out of his room. Then it was time to eat lunch.

"She called both boys to the table, but the younger brother, who was still crying, didn't hear her. He was still pitching his fit. After the older brother was done with his meal, his mother brought in the cake, with frosting and the candies sprinkled all over it, and a little scoop of ice cream.

"'Thank you for being patient and trusting that I had something good for you at the right time. Those candies were for the cake all along and I wanted you to have it all, not just part of it!' she said to the older brother, and she kissed him. Then she went into the younger brother's room, where he had finally calmed down. 'Do you know that I had food for you?' she asked.

"'I don't want food!' he cried.

"'You can come out, as soon as you're done crying. I wish you knew how much I love you, and how much I love to give you good things.' But he wouldn't listen. And he wouldn't come out of his room. And he never got the cake she made him."

After I told this story to my oldest son, I said, "Now Joshua, it's okay if you're still the little brother, but I'm excited for you to become mature, to learn patience and self-discipline, so you can have the blessings that we want to give you when you trust us."

"I will be the big brother, Momma," he replied. "And it's okay that I can't have the candy. I know you love me."

He doesn't always get it, and doesn't always say this when we tell him no. But when he does remember, I melt. I realize he is maturing.

Maturity is learning to tell your feelings, "Hey, feelings, just relax. Trust and be patient. Don't pitch a fit." It's learning to love discipline and obedience, to see the boundaries as freedom to do the right things at the right time. To see interruptions and changes in the way I thought things should or would go as an adventure. I had to learn to embrace the limitations so I could master my surroundings in such a way that tough life circumstances didn't have to always touch me deeply. Love, trust, self-control, and obedience are powerful armor.

During this time of growth, I was learning, within the boundaries of God's Word and within my relationship with Eric and Sarah, to say, "Okay, God, I know you love me. I know these boundaries exist to protect me." What powerful freedom! Being able to say this allowed me to move on in the hope that God had something better for me. It taught me to embrace what was in front of me as best as I could.

Learning the Beauty of Obedience

Maturity was celebrated in the Patricks' house by how you learned obedience. Obedience wasn't desired for religiosity's sake or for control. Obedience was celebrated because it showed the maturity of love and trust. It showed the beauty of being a daughter and a son.

Obedience brings joy. Disobedience brings some type of pain: emotional, spiritual, or the least type of pain, physical. This is what they taught their young, natural children. But as an adult, spiritual child of theirs, the more I willingly obeyed Eric and Sarah, out of love for and trust in God first and them second, the more I found joy and miraculous blessings.

Although I found hope in renewing my mind through the Bible, I didn't find joy until I learned obedience—obedience to the Scriptures and obedience to the gentle suggestions of my spiritual parents. It was such a magical adventure. I found the sweetest freedom within certain boundaries. And within that freedom I found another sweet magic. I began to love life.

I eventually found Eric and Sarah's house to be the place I felt the safest. But it was definitely a process. I struggled between having an *orphan mentality* and learning to *become a daughter*. I called God my heavenly Father, but until I learned how the heart of the Father is toward his children, I couldn't relate to him as a daughter.

Jesus said, "If you love me, *you will* obey my commandments."[2]

It wasn't him saying, "Love me *by* obeying me." Rather he was saying, "When you truly love me, you will want to obey, and you actually will obey. Obedience is not how you love me, it's the evidence that you truly love me."

What a revelation!

During my affair, I made grand speeches about how much I loved God, but honestly, I loved my own ideas *about* love. I loved my own ideas about "God" more than I loved God himself. I loved the emotional highs I got from feeling smart enough to justify my disobedience more than I loved Jesus. It wasn't until I began to choose obedience that I really began to love God for who he really is, within the covenant he intended for me to.

Never Meet Your Heroes

I had lunch with my friend Andrea one day after church. She loves Jesus so much and is a mother in the faith to me. Over soup and deli sandwiches, she told me the story of her first crush. She was infatuated with a boy at school. She thought about him constantly. She wrote him poems every day. She talked about him to her friends. She thought about him the first thing in the morning and just before falling asleep. But they never spoke to each other.

One fateful day, he happened to sit at her table for lunch. She was so nervous she could hardly stand it. But as the boy began to eat his lunch, everything changed. He ate so loudly that she found him revolting. She couldn't get over the way he chewed his food—she could hear everything going on in his mouth. It completely grossed her out. Her months of desperate infatuation were completely over. She was now disillusioned. She picked up her tray and walked to another table.

We talked about how often this is the way things play out with our emotions and feelings. There is a saying that goes, "Never meet your heroes." We can idolize someone, but when we meet them they totally crush our hearts by being a regular and perhaps even revolting human.

We also talked about how often this happens in an affair. People often quote the saying, "The grass is always greener on the other side" as a warning to people who have this illusion that someone else will be better as long as he or she isn't the person you're already with, whom you have gotten used to and know all the things you couldn't have known when you didn't live with them every day. So you begin to idolize the person you can't have. And many times the new relationship ends up with the same "issues" as the old one. The truth is the grass is greener where you water it. Idolizing people is only a recipe for heartbreak.

But then my friend Andrea said something I found strange. She said one day she was worshiping and telling the Lord how much she loved him, and this question came into her mind: *Lord, am I idealizing you in such a way that once I actually come to be with you, I will find I was only in love with an* idea *of you? Will I be disillusioned by you and not feel in love with you anymore?*

When she said this I thought, *This lady is one of the smartest people I know. Doesn't she know that the reason everyone else fails in this way is because they aren't Jesus and that's what we are really searching for all along? But once we have Jesus we discover that he is flawless—nothing to reject?*

But then she said something that made so much sense to me.

"The Lord spoke to my heart and showed me that the answer was *no*. He assured me I was not idealizing him the way I did with others. If I was only in love with an idea of him, then whenever he wanted me to do something I didn't want to do, I would not obey and I would walk away. He showed me that I've had many opportunities to walk away as I've gotten to know him and who he really is and what he really desires for me. But because I have obeyed, letting him shape my heart and change the way I think and live, even when it was difficult, I can see for myself that I really do love the Lord himself and not just my own ideas of him."

I was amazed at how well her illustration was able to teach me about true love and idealism. When I choose to be a daughter out of love for who God *really* is, I will obey him.

I will begin to see that his way really is the best way.

That's when I am the freest to be who I am created to be.

That's when I have stopped settling for less than all he wants for me.

That's when I begin to see this life as an adventure and begin to see his blessing, protection, and provision all around me.

Whenever I felt God closing a door to something I thought I wanted, or saying *no* to something I wanted him to say *yes* to, I would get excited because I knew he had something better. Instead of responding as an orphan and holding that door open because I thought I knew best, or instead of trying to justify why the *no* he gave really could still be a *yes* with my logic and manipulation, I began to let God be God. I quit trying to be God for others. I began to be a daughter. Whenever the Scriptures said, "No, that isn't good for you," or "No, you can't help them right now," I would say, "Okay, Daddy, I know you love me." And I would do it with so much joy.

Andrea Danko

Meet Andrea Danko. She is a hero to me because her greatest joy is getting to love God. I rarely see Andrea without a smile, unless she is travailing in prayer with passion and confidence. She is the most mature, most childlike, most stable, and most fluid person I know.

Here is a note to you, from Andrea.

Dear Reader,

Life is so much bigger and more awesome than we can ever imagine! True life is walking with Jesus every moment of the day, enjoying him and the adventures he has chosen personally just for us. We walk in a physical body, but we are heavenly beings who have the awesome calling to bring heaven down on earth. This is our true identity, which we must never forget. Life in and with Jesus never ends, so relax. Don't take yourself too seriously and never give up! Every hard time will pass, and great is the reward of those who finish the race. Things that don't make sense today will tomorrow. Everything shapes and molds us according to the ever-loving heart and intentions of our heavenly Father.

With the heavenly Father's love,

Andrea Danko,
wife, mom, professor, pastor, intercessor

Relationships are not sustained through singular or random moments. They are carved out in the splintered beauty of the everyday, one day stacked on another.

17

THE MYSTERY OF
Marrying Jesus

For your Maker is your husband, the LORD of hosts is
his name; and the Holy One of Israel is your Redeemer,
the God of the whole earth he is called.

Isaiah 54:5 ESV

As I waved goodbye through the screen door the warm
Texas air played with the bottom of my favorite twirly
dress. The multicolored Andy Warhol poster of Einstein stick-
ing his tongue out quietly rattled on the wall as I closed my
front door.

The smell of hot peach cobbler lingered in the dining room after
all my guests had left. Ella Fitzgerald was still singing of her love
outlasting the Rocky Mountains. The taste of Earl Grey lingered
in my mouth and reminded me of the beautiful conversation I'd

just had with Lori over a cup of hot tea. I dropped onto the retro green couch I'd found at a thrift store and let out a sigh.

It had been a long, lovely evening. My heart was flooded with thankfulness. The big gold lamp sitting on the end table above my head lit up the floor, from the cherry hardwood that flowed from the living room to the dining room all the way to the black-and-white-checkered floor in the kitchen. I loved this house. Within the past three years, my band had been signed, toured the world, and made enough money for me to buy my own house.

I felt a wave of giddiness tickle my heart and talked to God out loud. "Thank you, Daddy," I whispered through a goofy smile.

I closed my eyes and remembered one of the apartments I'd lived in with my siblings growing up. We could barely fit two mattresses on the floor in the living room of the efficiency apartment. Even if we owned one, which we didn't, there was no room for a sofa in that tiny place. I stretched out my legs on my beautiful couch and said again, out loud to God, "Thank you, Daddy."

It was a strange thing to feel like a woman in that moment. To celebrate feeling like a grown-up, I'd worn red lipstick and high heels to my party. There's something about hosting a party, at your own house, that makes you feel grown-up. I started thinking about all the things my mom used to say about being a woman.

One time, when I was about thirteen, I was watching a TV show at my aunt's house in which a young girl had slept with her boyfriend. The girl's friend said to her, with a tinge of jealousy in her voice, "Well, how does it feel to officially be a real woman now?" My mom happened to walk by and stopped to watch part of the scene. She made a face of disgust at the comment and talked to the TV like the girls could hear her. "Having sex doesn't make you a woman, little girl! Lacey, I don't want you watching this garbage. Go in the other room."

Embarrassed at my mom's reaction, I secretly rolled my eyes as I left the room.

But here I was, in this moment, feeling all grown-up. And as I thought about that moment and my mother's words, I kept tripping over the question. *What does it mean to be a woman?*

I thought about the last conversation I'd had with my ex-husband. One night, after we'd been divorced for over a year, he unexpectedly dropped in.

"I'm sorry I wasn't completely honest with you when we got married. I'm not sure I even knew how to be honest, really, though," I told him during our conversation.

"I'm sorry I didn't try to save the marriage like I should have," he admitted. "But Lacey, we were so young!"

Yes. I could agree with that. Married at nineteen, divorced at twenty-one. Looking back, I guess I didn't know what it meant to be a woman when I got married the first time.

But what about now? I was single. I was happy. I felt thankful. I felt free.

I also recognized that only a couple years earlier there had been hidden snags in my heart that led me to foolish heartbreak. So what about now? Could there be more things within me that would keep me from being the woman I wanted to be?

What kind of woman did I want to be anyway?

What did it mean to be a woman?

I wasn't sure.

I Am Woman, a Mystery

I opened my eyes and stared at the ceiling. The lamplight cast a huge shadow in the corner. I followed the line of where light met shadow all the way down the wall, across the floor, and up the coffee table. On top of the table lay a book I had never read. It was a gift someone had brought to the party for me. The shadow drew a line right underneath the title of the book, like the lamp meant to underline it. *The Proust Questionnaire.*

The font was gold, embossed, like it was from another decade. I sat up, grabbed the book, and opened it to a random page. The first thing I read was a question. "What quality do you admire most in a woman?" My stomach flipped at the mystical way I was reading a book addressing the same topic I had been lying there contemplating. There was a line after the question with handwritten scribble on it. I could barely make it out. The word began with an "m" and ended with a "y."

I flipped through the pages and found that there were many of these questionnaires through the book, answered by different famous people. I looked up the same question in as many places I could find it, and over and over the answer was the same. What quality do you most admire in a woman? *Mystery.*

The consistency intrigued me. As I pondered this while sitting on my green couch, I realized I had read something the day before that reminded me of this intriguing answer. I grabbed my journal, opened to yesterday's entry, and found this version of 1 Peter 3:3–5 written at the top of the page:

"Let your beauty not come from outward adornment but from the hidden, inner person of the heart. For this is how women of old made themselves beautiful, not given to fear but having a gentle and quiet spirit."

What did all this mean?

I lay down with a restless heart that night. *What kind of woman am I going to be? What kind of woman am I made to be? What does it mean to be a mystery, or to be hidden? What is a quiet spirit, and how is that the result of not being given to fear? What does that look like in real life, now, today?*

The Day I Married Jesus

One day I was reading the Scriptures and came across an interesting passage in the book of Isaiah. In it, God speaks to a barren woman who was cast off by her husband when she was young. He reminds her, "Your Maker is your husband" (Isa. 54:5). When I read this my heart leapt, so I kept reading. Further in the passage God calls the land of Israel *Beulah*. And *beulah* in Hebrew means "married." I cried, thinking about letting go of romance altogether and committing to never marry anyone else. Nuns do this all the time, right? Was there a non-Catholic way to commit your life to God and never marry? I'd never heard of such a thing. But that didn't stop me from coming up with my own version of a non-Catholic, rock-and-roll nunnery.

I called my friend Zach, who is a tattoo artist, and booked an appointment for Friday. I sent out a text to all my friends and family, inviting them to dinner at my house after I got my tattoo. I felt a strange sense of peace as I mentally prepared for this celebratory dinner party. I was going to have a tattoo wedding service, with a dinner reception at my house that I would prepare. It felt so right.

Meanwhile, I had been reading where Jesus said, "If you love me then you will obey me" (see John 14:15). This was my heart's desire—to purposely love Jesus in this way. So I made it my goal. I scoured the New Testament, noted all the direct commands of Jesus, and wrote them down. Jesus gives the most commands in the Sermon on the Mount in Matthew 5–7. I took the full-length mirror I had hanging on the door to my bedroom and wrote out all the direct commands from that sermon. My plan was to look at one command a day and focus on loving Jesus by obeying it intentionally that day.

Day 1: *Rejoice and be glad when people insult me because of my love for God.*

Day 2: *Let my light shine with good deeds in front of others.*

Day 3: *Do not be angry with my brother.*

Day 4: *Reconcile with any brother who had something against me.*

Day 5: *Resolve conflicts with friends, family, or coworkers right away.*

Day 6: *Don't purposefully lust after anyone.* I had learned from my affair that, for me, this included emotional lust as well as physical.

Day 7: *Remove whatever causes me to sin that is obvious.* I did not mean physically gouging my eye out, but rather I believe Jesus was using a metaphor here, letting us know that even if that thing is as important to you as your eyes, or as your right arm, you are to cut it off, gouge it out, and throw it away.

I worked on obeying this list of Jesus's commands daily. I also committed to reading Proverbs 31 daily. I wanted to learn what a wife of noble character looked like. My desire was to make this "wife of noble character" a pattern for my life as a bride of Christ. Who was she?

She was diligent and did her work eagerly.

She had food ready for those whom she was to feed, and food for me meant spiritual food like Scriptures and encouragement.

She got up while it was still night to provide food for her family. So I would purposefully think of ways to encourage my friends and family and feed their souls with thoughtfulness and kindness and love.

She made good business decisions and found purposeful ways to use her finances that were smart and responsible and would grow them. She was physically fit and healthy, and strong and able to do whatever task she needed to.

She didn't consider sleep more important than the adventure of loving people and serving them and she was excited to do that. She was generous and helpful and had no fear of not having provision. She thought ahead. She dressed in a lovely way that would be appropriate for royalty.

I looked at these descriptions and prayed about how they fit with my life, and how I could become this type of a bride to the Lord.

That Friday, I wore a white dress. I invited my friend Lori to come with me, and I laughed with her as Zach engraved the word *beulah* on my left arm with ink. There I was, the bride in the white dress, committing myself forever to my Maker, my husband. My tattoo was my ring, and my joy a healing salve.

That evening I came home, put on worship music, and danced around my apartment. I made salmon, rice, and vegetables for dinner with salad and fresh homemade strawberry lemonade. I picked flowers for the table and lit scented candles. Right before my friends came over, I switched the music from worship to some '30s and '40s jazz. I felt like my worship time was just between me and the Lord. I didn't tell anyone why I was celebrating; I just focused on loving them and serving them.

Our Hidden Wonder

Earlier that week I'd read in the Scriptures about how women of old made themselves beautiful to God by submitting to their husbands, and how the beauty of a woman should come first from the hidden person of the heart, the unfading beauty of a gentle and quiet spirit, which is of great worth in God's sight (see 1 Pet. 3:3–5).

I was fascinated by the phrase "hidden person of the heart." I looked up *hidden* in my concordance and found it in another place that sounded intriguing. "For you have died, and your life is *hidden* with Christ in God" (Col. 3:3 ESV). It was as if in the same way that a wife would keep her body hidden and reserved for her husband, a woman would be beautiful to God by hiding her heart away, reserving it for the Lord, even and especially when she was married. I didn't understand it completely, but my mind began to rest on the idea and turn it over and over in my thoughts.

I kept it all in mind as I focused on loving my guests. I gushed with joy but I kept the reason for my joy to myself. I made my conversation always about what was going on in the lives of my guests. Serving them with my "husband" Jesus, who washed his disciples' feet and ate dinner with them regularly.

To some, it may seem odd to commit to daily doing the things that Jesus commands. But to me it felt like falling in love—for real. I didn't follow Jesus's commands because I was being forced to; I followed them because my heart desired to know him more deeply. My soul yearned for him. The more I spent time in the Scriptures, the more joy I experienced in my daily life.

Intentional and consistent daily connection with God is powerful. He doesn't want once-a-week religious obedience; he wants a real, everyday relationship with each of us!

Relationships are not sustained through singular or random moments. They are carved out in the splintered beauty of the everyday, one day stacked on another. Here is where the mystery begins. Here is where I found myself, as he sees me.

Hero Note:
Nick Hall

Meet Nick Hall. He is a hero to me because he is an ordinary person who does extraordinary things. He simply found life in Jesus and clings to him daily. He is a profound example of a son, because he lays everything on the line to obey what he knows God has called him to do. His faith is powerful and contagious.

Here is a note to you, from Nick.

Dear Reader,

Jesus changes everything. I can have all the money in the world, all the fame, the biggest house, fastest car, and hottest wife; but if I don't have Jesus, I have nothing. He is the greatest source of hope, love, and purpose in human history and you can know him for yourself.

If I could, I'd go back and tell my teenage self, "Go all in for Jesus. Pray more. Read more. Share Jesus more. Stop any questionable habit and invest in eternity. Pray great prayers and take great risks for God. The best things in life are the moments defined by all-out surrender!"

With the Father's love,

Nick
husband, father, evangelist, founder of Pulse Ministries and the Reset Movement

There's something so freeing that comes when we understand that the God of the universe loves us, and that he demonstrated that love by sending Jesus. Man, I don't care what the world says about me, because I know what God says about me. And I know what he says about you. He loves us.

Nick Hall[1]

18

The Mystery of
Heavenly Attraction

And the angel said to me, "Write this: Blessed are those
who are invited to the marriage supper of the Lamb."
And he said to me, "These are the true words of God."
Then I fell down at his feet to worship him, but he said
to me, "You must not do that! I am a fellow servant
with you and your brothers who hold to the testimony
of Jesus. Worship God." For the testimony of Jesus is
the spirit of prophecy.

Revelation 19:9–10 ESV

I needed to figure out how to live out this "marriage to Jesus" in
a way that wouldn't get me tangled up in romance. I wanted
to give up romance altogether.

It turns out that this is one of the most attractive things to people:
someone who is whole. Someone who is healthy on their own. Someone who is happy and loves to serve others without expecting anything
in return. Being a mystery turns out to be attractive in a deeper way

than just physical beauty. It's more beautiful than charm or wit or humor. It's attractive because it shines with the light of Jesus. And, as I learned from my encounter with God when I asked him how to move on and leave behind the affair and all the ways I was tangled up in that person, God showed me that the only thing I loved in Nathan was Jesus. And the only thing Nathan loved in me was Jesus.

Many times, the closer you get to Jesus, the more people want to be close to you. Many times they will mistake Jesus's light in you for your own light. As they fall in love with Jesus they may feel they are falling in love with you. So how do you stay single and become that mystery, hidden away in Christ while still outwardly loving and serving everyone around you with freedom and joy—and still shine in the beautiful way that you were meant to shine without having people mistake his light for yours? How do you let his supernatural beauty flow through you without having people become infatuated with you?

And when they have romantic feelings toward you because of the light of Christ, how do you not feel the warmth of their admiration? How do you guard yourself against falling in love too? How can you ever stay committed to singleness and loving Christ when loving him makes you so beautiful that people fall in love with you? Loving him makes you love people so deeply, but how can you be sure not to mistake his *eternal, heavenly,* and *godly* love for *temporal, earthly,* and *romantic* love?

How do you live in purity when you are committed to never getting married? How do you have purity in your relationships with brothers and sisters? I had a hard time finding answers to these questions in the Scriptures.

How Do I Live in Purity?

One obvious answer was to learn how to treat people as brothers and sisters, and to generally stick more with my sisters than my brothers. But I felt certain I was called into a male-dominated industry. So how would I do this well?

I fasted and prayed about this for a few days, and a couple things happened. The first one was that I was working on the part in the Sermon on the Mount where Jesus says to let your *yes* be yes and your *no* be no (Matt. 5:37; see also James 5:12). I tried to focus on this command from Jesus and realized after two weeks of trying to complete one day of intentional obedience to this command that I could not do it—unless I stopped talking altogether! No matter how well intentioned I was, I could not control the circumstances that would change my *yes* to a no or my *no* to a yes, and I was struggling. And I hadn't even gotten to the command in Matthew 5 that says to be perfect!

The second thing that happened was that a passage of Scripture from Matthew 19 kept following me around. Jesus was talking to the religious experts of the day—the Pharisees—who were grilling him on the topic of divorce. Here's their conversation:

> Some Pharisees came to him to test him. They asked, "Is it lawful for a man to divorce his wife for any and every reason?"
>
> "Haven't you read," he replied, "that at the beginning the Creator made them 'male and female,' and said, 'For this reason a man will leave his father and mother and be united to his wife, and the two will become one flesh'? So they are no longer two, but one flesh. Therefore, what God has joined together, let no one separate.'"
>
> "Why then," they asked, "did Moses command that a man give his wife a certificate of divorce and send her away?"
>
> Jesus replied, "Moses permitted you to divorce your wives because your hearts were hard. But it was not this way from the beginning. I tell you that anyone who divorces his wife, except for sexual immorality, and marries another woman commits adultery."
>
> The disciples said to him, "If this is the situation between a husband and a wife, it is better not to marry."

Jesus replied, "Not everyone can accept this word, but only those to whom it has been given. For there are eunuchs who were born that way, and there are eunuchs who have been made eunuchs by others—and there are those who choose to live like eunuchs for the sake of the kingdom of heaven. The one who can accept this should accept it." (vv. 3–12)

Two things got my attention about this.

First, I noticed Jesus was always trying to show the religious people how their best efforts in following the law always fell short. They thought they obeyed the law by getting a divorce in the proper way, but Jesus told them the legitimate reasons for divorce were very specific. During this time, men would write off their wives for any and every reason, and this would socially disgrace and ruin a woman. These people weren't committing to loving someone in a covenant way.

God's permission for divorce was a grace—an allowance. He would rather people separate than abuse one another, because he has called us to live in peace. But these Pharisees were only concerned with the letter of the law, not the heart of God. God wanted the marriage covenant to be kept so the covenant would force people to work through the hard times. God desires that we never give up growing together and learning how to *really* love.

The specific reasons for divorce are evidence of God's compassion. When people experience hard, abusive, unloving, unmovable hearts in their marriage, God gives grace. He doesn't want that type of religious control to represent what marriage is supposed to be. God wants us to enter and maintain our marriages with soft hearts.

In this passage, Jesus exposed their religiosity and their lack of understanding when it came to God's heart. Their hearts did not desire purity. They just wanted to justify their sinful actions. They committed adultery and drew up divorce papers, believing they were doing what was required of them. Some of them went to the other extreme and never married, thinking that was super spiritual. But again, their motives were not pure.

What about me? I was married once. My heart grew unfaithful. I fell in love with another man while I was married. I was like the Pharisees: religious minus the heart of God. But my repentance was sharp—I was teetering on an extreme reaction, like the Pharisees yet again. I no longer desired a romantic relationship. But maybe it was more than that. Maybe deep down I didn't think I had the *right* to be in a romantic relationship. I wanted to know God's heart. I desired purity. But how?

On top of it all, I was having trouble with my list—you know, the one I made where I focused on obeying one thing each day that Jesus instructed us to do. The one that really got me was "Let your yes be yes." No matter how hard I tried, I kept failing at this one. A heavy feeling loomed over my heart and whispered to me, *You can't carry this out even for a day—you're a sinner and you will never stop sinning. Who do you think you are to imagine you could ever love God?*

Those whispers accused me by bringing up the emotional affair I had barely survived. During that time I had such a scare with the depth of my sin, and now I wanted nothing to do with it. I wanted to be rid of it forever. I curled up in my bed and wept. I just wanted to stop sinning! I felt like I could never obey God or love him well; I would always do the thing I didn't want to do. I wanted to go to heaven—no temptation there, no sin, no shame or sorrow.

I looked down at my wrist and followed the blue line of vein down my arm and felt another whisper of the enemy. I could tell he was trying to be poetic. The clever devil knew I was a sucker for poetry. I remembered Peter Pan's words, "Death would be a great adventure." That sounded profound and inviting to me as I thought through the question of whether or not God would let me come to heaven if I took my life. The thought was very short, and I don't know if it was my own thought or the enemy's. I yelled "Shut up!" into my pillow anyway.

I got up and wrote a verse on my wrist, all the way down my arm, from 1 Corinthians 6:19–20: "*You are not your own; you were bought at a price.*" I reread the verses in Matthew about marriage and the question from the Pharisees, and the disciples' reaction: "It is better not to marry" (Matt. 19:10).

I began to ask myself, *Was my decision to never marry given to me by God, like Jesus mentioned? Or is it just a religious pendulum swing in an attempt to fix my sin and punish myself in some way? Am I going on with this singleness because God has called me to it? Or am I just trying to do something I wasn't called to?*

Clearly I was to embrace, at the very least, a season of singleness. It was a gift from God. I was enjoying and appreciating it. But I wanted to know if my commitment to marrying Jesus and never marrying anyone else was being like the religious people whom Jesus was always correcting. He was trying to show them they would never be righteous by trying to keep all the commandments. That's why Jesus came. He came to keep all the commands that we could never keep.

Never Perfect, Always Loved

When we really examine ourselves, we will find that we can never obey God completely by our own efforts. It's like if we had a microscope, we would find that we can never be clean no matter how much we clean ourselves. Or it's like cleaning our house. We can never *completely* clean it no matter how hard we try. The more we try, the more we find to do. We can never do things perfectly before God. That's the reality. But that truth is not meant to make us work harder to be perfect or give up on following the Lord. Quite the opposite, in fact.

It's meant to humble us.

It's meant to show us that our very lives depend on God's love and grace.

It's meant to make us fall in love with the One who loves us, despite all our failures and mistakes.

His deep love compels us to love him back. And the *evidence* of our love will be displayed in a lovesick obedience. His deep love assures us that even in our disobedience we're never far from his love—we can never lose it. It was wrong for the religious people to think that their letter-of-the-law living could win them salvation. God did not give us his Word, through the Scriptures, for us to live bound and gagged. He gave us his Word so we'd fall in love with him. In the book of Deuteronomy God instructed the Israelites to always meditate on his commandments day and night. To talk about them and teach them to their children. Why? Because the more they examined the commandments, the more they would find themselves in need of forgiveness and a savior.

Notice that word *need*. When you and I come to the point where we can honestly say we *need* something, we arrive at a place of humility. God's law draws us in because it is altogether good. Meditating on this goodness reveals how we can never truly be good by the law's perfect standard. Maybe that's why Jesus commanded us to "Be perfect" (Matt. 5:48). Maybe he wanted to let the religious Pharisees give up their mask of pretending to be holy and admit that they were sinners.

The orphan mindset does not think this way. I had a constant tendency to try to earn my keep. It's only sons and daughters who get the free gifts and inheritance. I didn't want this whole struggle to become something rooted in an orphan mindset that couldn't receive the free gift of forgiveness paid for by Christ's blood shed on the cross.

I was thinking through this when I prayed quietly.

A Daughter's Prayer

Lord, please protect my heart from the lies of the enemy. I don't want to become some religious person whom you have to rebuke harshly in front of everyone so that you can protect the people you love from condemnation and a false-gospel way of thinking that says we can earn our forgiveness by "good" works.

Don't let me get mixed-up or deceived. You know I don't think I can make myself righteous by staying single, but please don't let me try without even realizing it. I don't want to deceive myself. Please show me if I am one of the ones you've given the gift of singleness to or not. If I am one of those, please teach me how to be pure in my relationships, so I can guard my own heart and honor the hearts of those you have put around me.

Fasting and Writing the List

I continued my fast.

Every day I read Isaiah 58 about what a true fast is. During the day I did my best to serve whoever was in front of me. I was generous every chance I got, and as I served and loved the people around me I was filled with joy. I committed to not eat until 7:00 p.m. every day, and right before I ate I went to be alone somewhere and pray.

Once I was at a friend's house and went upstairs to pray before dinner. As I went to lay my face on the floor in front of a bookshelf, I saw a book that caught my eye. *The Bride Wore White.* I had read several Christian dating books, like *Passion and Purity*, *Lady in Waiting*, and others. I learned a little from each one. Some stuff I liked and related to. Some stuff I hated and couldn't relate to at all.

But when I saw the book was about "purity in relationships," I thought it might actually address what I was curious about. I borrowed it and brought it home, but realized quickly that it was all about romance. I almost put it down, because I wanted to know how to have purity in *all* relationships, not dating ones. I still had no desire to date. But it seemed like a quick read, so I went ahead and started reading it.

When I got to the chapter about writing a list of what I wanted in a husband, I totally skipped it. But after I did that, I saw that the following chapter made references to the list chapter, so I put the book down altogether.

The next day I picked it up and the pages fell open to the list chapter. My eyes somehow locked on the first sentence of the chapter and it was a quote from someone who had read the book before. She said, "I didn't want to make this list, because I didn't want to get married . . ." I laughed out loud.

Okay, God, I thought, rolling my eyes. *I'll read this chapter.* So I did. And I decided to make the list. I was so adamant in my mind that I didn't want to be married, and I was hoping my fast would reveal that God had called me to a single life, so I decided I would make the list ridiculous. Practically unanswerable. It was so detailed, and it went on and on and on. I came up with sixty things. They were as specific as meaningful tattoos, freckles close up, random beauty marks, hazel eyes, and "I don't care" hair, and as broad as loves Jesus and metal music, loves philosophy and art, plays guitar, is shy and will pursue me even though I'm a rock star. At the end of it all, I made sure to include a stipulation that would ensure any resulting match would be miraculous, and the last line of the list read: "If I ever found a guy who fit the list completely, he would have to chase me even if I ignored him."

19

THE MYSTERY OF
the One

Record the vision and inscribe it on tablets, That the
one who reads it may run. For the vision is yet for
the appointed time; It hastens toward the goal and it
will not fail. Though it tarries, wait for it; for it will
certainly come, it will not delay.

Habakkuk 2:2–3 NASB

A few months later, in the springtime of 2007, we were
doing a headline tour across the United States. We were
playing a show at Rocket Town in Nashville when I saw *him*.

He had the "I don't care" hair. He had tattoos. This guy met
so many of the physical traits on my list, even the hazel eyes. So,
naturally, I tried to stay hidden on the bus. But every time I came
out he seemed to be around. I'd mentioned my list to our assistant
tour manager, Katy, and she noticed right away that he fit.

"You should give him your number."

"No, Katy, that's not how this works."

"What do you mean?"

"He has to chase me. I'm not gonna make anything happen. It has to be organic. I can't manipulate. I don't want to get married anyway. I don't need a boyfriend."

"Lacey, give him your number, or I will."

"No, I'm serious, don't do that, Katy."

"I'm gonna do it. You need me to help you."

"Katy, if you give him my number I will fire you."

We both laughed and she quit badgering me.

By the end of the night, I was relieved to discover he was not the one I'd written about. I danced around the bus as we pulled away from the venue because he hadn't asked for my number. I was thanking God for the list. "He's not the one! I don't have to get married!"

I acted juvenile in my joy. I really could see the benefit and safety of having a list, even though I had made fun of the idea in my head. I remember when my friend Kat met her husband, Jared, she'd said, "I'll just be so excited if he's not the one, because that means God has someone better than him, and I just can't even fathom that."

I completely understood what she meant as I hopped around the bus.

Josh!

One month later our tour took us through Ohio. A girl named Kendyll, whom we had met a while back, came to see us. She was a young band manager. I remembered her because she was extraordinarily beautiful and full of joy.

I was happy she was there. She brought two people along with her I didn't know. One was a reserved music teacher. The other was the guitarist from Kairos, the band she managed. I saw him standing with everyone outside the bus window. So I went out to greet them. The first thing I noticed when I walked up were his tattoos. There was an angel on his left forearm. She was hovering over a bird. The bird had babies and blood on her beak.

The conversation carried on and I quietly asked this guy with the tattoos about his arm.

"What does that mean?"

"This? Oh, it's the symbolism of the pelican. They use it in a lot of Catholic paintings and imagery to represent Christ. The legend goes that during a time of famine, a mother pelican will open her stomach with her beak and let the babies eat her flesh and drink her blood, so they can survive while she dies. So like Christ, she gives her life so they can live."

My heart fluttered as he talked about his meaningful tattoo. I looked up at him and wondered if I should walk away. If he fit the list, I would have. But beneath the shadow of his shaggy, shoulder length, light brown "I don't care" hair he had brown eyes. My heart relaxed and I realized I could be friendly. I wouldn't compromise on the eye color just because I wanted to find any pitiful excuse to not get married. As the conversation popcorned in the circle, the topic of metal bands came up.

"I started a Pantera fan club in high school," he said, and laughed. I felt a rush of heat come over my face and I giggled. *He loves Jesus and he likes metal music. That's so lovely*, I thought to myself. I went on to tell him about being from Arlington, Texas, where Pantera started, and how my brother and I would try to learn their songs on the bass and guitar in junior high.

Things started to get busy backstage and I had to get ready for the show, so I didn't see him again for a few hours. Later we were all hanging out on the bus, and Sameer seemed to be in a philosophical conversation with him. Then Kendyll called his name. "Josh! Here, Scotty gave me these passes so they'll let us go backstage."

His name is Joshua. One of my favorite names. I smiled to myself while I eavesdropped on him and Sameer talking about parallel universes and black holes. My heart was becoming more and more enchanted by this mysterious guy.

I started to pray for his wife. I know not everyone is called to marriage, but I kept thinking of the verse, "It's not good for a man to be alone" whenever I heard him speak. So I prayed for whomever God would lead him to marry. He was not dating Kendyll, that was clear.

He was quiet and reserved, but seemed to have a lot on his mind. I prayed that his future wife would appreciate his love for metal and his passion for music. I prayed that she would appreciate his interest in philosophy and the mystical nature of the universe. I prayed that she would honor his reserved, quiet shyness but also be able to bring out the playful heart that he also seemed to carry beneath all the weight of his thoughts. I prayed that I would honor her, whoever she was, in the way I treated him during our little encounter.

Even though he kept hitting points on my list, I kept telling myself he wasn't the one. Because his eyes were brown. It's true the list chapter in *The Bride Wore White* specifically said to be flexible with physical traits, but I was too happy being single! I wasn't interested in romance with a guy. I was already swept off my feet and enjoying a captivating romance with Life itself. So I ignored the book's leniency.

But my heart was filled with God's love for Joshua and how specially he seemed to be wired. I wanted God's best for him and prayed that for him. I prayed that he would fulfill all God had created him to accomplish. I didn't talk to him again until the show was over. When I got to the bus, I kicked off my shoes before I realized Josh and his friends were leaving. I thought maybe I could catch them before they drove off, so I jumped out of the bus and was walking barefoot across the parking lot when my tour manager, Scotty Rock, saw me.

"Oh, come on, where are your shoes, Lace?" he asked, annoyed.

"Did you see where Sameer and James's friends went?" I asked, ignoring his question.

"This is a bar parking lot. There's probably glass and broken bottles all over the place out here," he said as he turned around, knelt down, and pulled my arms around his neck, then stood up to his full six-foot-something height. He started to go back toward the bus while I protested.

"But I want to look for that group of people that were on the bus earlier. I want to invite them to hang out."

"Who are you talking about?"

"Look! I think I see them! I think that's them getting into their car."

Scotty shifted course to head toward that car.

"Just tell them they can stay if they want," I said. I was a bit nervous because it seemed like I was trying to chase them down.

"Who are they again?"

My mind went blank on everyone's name but Josh.

"The one girl's name starts with a K, but the guy's name is Josh."

"Josh!" Scotty's loud, deep voice rang out across the parking lot. I buried my head against Scotty's shoulder. I was mortified. Now it really looked like I was chasing him. Immediately I remembered the girl's name was Kendyll. Why couldn't I remember two seconds ago?

I saw them look up. Three silhouettes. Then slowly they closed the car doors and began to walk back across the parking lot. My feelings ricocheted. Embarrassment. Excitement. More embarrassment. But mostly, I was happy we could all hang out a little longer.

The Dream Giver and Hazel Eyes

Since our bus call was at 2:00 a.m. and the venue had no showers, we had reserved one hotel room to shower in. The whole band and crew piled into the tiny space, covering the beds, the floor, and a couple of chairs as we all took turns getting showers. Josh sat on the floor and the whole room buzzed with conversation. My friend Ryan's band, Resident Hero, was on tour with us at the time, and Ryan was sitting on one end of the bed beside his drummer and I was sitting on other end. I stretched out my legs in front of me. I wore pajama shorts that went down to my knees and a big, baggy T-shirt.

Ryan was absentmindedly staring at my legs while he talked to his drummer about something and then stopped midsentence, leaned his face in close to my shins, and announced loudly in joking disgust, "Lacey, girl, you need to shave them legs! You are a hairy little monkey."

I rolled my eyes at his roasting humor, but wondered if I had grossed out our guests. I was surprised to feel embarrassed, because I had been so free of that feeling for so long. I immediately embraced the embarrassing moment and settled into it as safety. I realized I didn't want to wear any mask and I didn't want to feel like I needed to defend myself either. So I laughed with Ryan at his joke.

Josh had mentioned that Kendyll was the manager for his band, so I asked what instrument he played.

"Guitar. But the band is broken up now. I'm not really sure what I should do now. I have so many songs I've written, but I don't know what I'm supposed to do with them all."

"Have you ever heard of a book called *The Dream Giver* by Bruce Wilkinson?" I asked.

"No," he answered.

"It's a short allegory about a guy who wants to follow his dreams but only gets them after he gives them up. I really liked it."

"Maybe I'll check it out."

I noticed his worn-out Converse All-Stars had been dyed and written on, so I pulled a Sharpie out of my backpack and said, "I can write it on your shoe, so you don't forget?"

He pulled himself up and sat on the edge of the bed, and situated himself so I could write on it.

"THE DREAM GIVER," I wrote in all caps.

I looked up at his smiling face and at that moment someone stepped out of the lamplight and the light hit Josh's eyes. The hazel green I hadn't been able to see earlier glowed from his eyes like fire going right into my heart. I looked down at my bag, flustered.

I put my Sharpie away and turned my attention to a girl named Mia. Realizing that now I had lost the sad little excuse I was hanging on to for why he didn't fit my list, my mind raced as I talked to Mia and tried to focus on her.

"So what instrument do you play, Mia?"

"Piano mostly, but I can play the violin too. I teach voice as well."

"And you teach children?"

"Yes."

"I love kids so much. I never get to be around them, being on tour," I said, trying to turn so I couldn't see Josh in my peripheral vision.

I kept thinking about my commitment to not manipulate or chase a man if he seemed to fit my list. I tried my best to completely withdraw from my conversation with Josh, but we had already talked so much. And we connected so easily. I marveled at how I hadn't been able to tell the color of his eyes until now. I thought back through our conversation and wondered about how personal I'd been, questioning whether I'd been too friendly.

Then I heard Scotty announce it was time for bus call. Kendyll, Josh, and Mia all stood up and went to the door.

"Well, it was fun hanging out," he said.

"Yeah, it was nice to meet you," I answered.

I wondered whether he would ask for my number.

After he shut the door to the hotel room, I exhaled. He didn't fit the last requirement. He didn't pursue me. I was so relieved! I knew that if he had pursued me, he may very well have been the one I'd written about. But since he didn't, I was free to pray for him and his future spouse and let him go, without any interruptions in my romance with Life.

I prayed that he would be safe on his drive home and that he would connect with God and be filled with hope for his future. I prayed that he would be creative and have outlets for his creativity and that God would connect him with the right people so that he would have joy and love and the fullness of life. I prayed God would use his gifts of guitar and music in ways that were glorious. And when I went to bed that night, I thanked God for my list and my boundaries. I thanked God for freedom from the feeling of needing to manipulate a love story into unfolding. I thanked God that he had good plans and a future for me and that he was kind and had perfect timing. I thanked him that *his ways were the best ways*. I fell asleep with such joy and peace in knowing that we can't mess up God's best for us if that is what we are seeking with all our hearts.

Morning Date with Jesus and Noah

The next day I woke up before anyone else. We had a show that night in Louisville at a club called Headliners. The bus had made the five-and-a-half-hour journey while we slept in our bunks and was now parked outside the venue. With 2:00 a.m. bedtimes, mornings were always quiet on the bus. When I pulled up the shade on one of the windows, the sun was shining soft and warm in the blue Kentucky sky. I giggled at its thoughtful beauty. I laughed because God is so intentional and beautiful, and it's just so romantic. A boyfriend may give you a candlelit dinner but God gives you a new sunrise every morning.

177

"Hi," I said out loud, toward the beauty that my beloved, heavenly King seemed to have poured into the sky just for me to rejoice in. I stuffed my Bible and journal into the hobo sack I'd received as a gift at a radio show we had done earlier that year, then I slipped the strap over my head, shifted the book-heavy pouch around to my back, and skipped to the front of the bus with a silly kind of joy. With no one else awake yet, it felt like I was sneaking off to be with my Love. I opened the bus door, then stood on the passenger seat and climbed up, putting one foot on the ledge by the handle, then the other high on the dashboard, then moving up to edge out of the window, until I finally pulled my body onto the roof. The metal bus roof was growing warm from the sun, so I laid my face on the surface and smiled.

"Hi," I said again to God.

I felt so much peace and love, I just wanted to laugh again. But just in case any crew or venue guys were wandering around below me, I was quiet so I could protect my alone time with God. I pulled my Bible out of my bag and laid it open in front of me, sat up on my elbows, and rested my chin on my fists in order to read. The sun was shining through my eyelashes and rainbows shot out from them in all directions. Something I wouldn't have noticed before I met Nathan. I closed my eyes and thanked God for making rainbows. I remembered to do as God had shown me that day I cried while looking into my trashcan, when I decided to believe in him despite my feelings or understanding. *Think of me when you see rainbows.*

He had spoken so sweetly to my heart.

I turned to the back of my Bible and looked up rainbows in the concordance. I read about how God told Noah that the rainbow was a sign to him and all creation that he would never again destroy the earth by a flood. Then I researched Noah. I read about him in Hebrews and First and Second Peter. I felt revelation washing over me as I prayed that the Holy Spirit would help me understand what I was reading and what it said about my own life and how to live and love.

I was flooded with God's love as I sat praying, thanking him again for the sunshine and this time alone with him. Then I sat still, just glowing with gratefulness. Thankful that I was single. Thankful that my heart was safe with God.

Your Maker Is Your Husband

God was more than enough for me. This I felt through and through. It occurred to me how others might respond if they knew I was having a date with God; I was sure they would think it strange that in my heart of hearts I was relating to God as a husband, but I was so utterly happy, so satisfied with him. He filled me with hope and joy and purpose. I could never reach the depths of his mystery and his love.

I also wondered why more people who called themselves Christians didn't take a time of singleness and, in a spiritual sense, marry Jesus. It was so glorious and it seemed to be such a shame to spend your single time waiting on some other person to fulfill you or complete you or be your purpose in life when there was so much life in being married to God in this way.

I also wondered, again, about the passages I had read about being single and staying unmarried. Was I being religious in the way I was shut off to romance in my life? Was I just afraid of being perceived by the world a certain way, or was I afraid that I would deceive myself or be rejected again? I had so much joy and fullness being single and being married to Jesus in my heart. But I questioned myself.

What exactly does that Scripture—Isaiah 54—say about your Maker being your husband? I asked myself, and I flipped to the passage and read the whole thing in context.

"Do not be afraid; you will not be put to shame.
    Do not fear disgrace; you will not be humiliated.
You will forget the shame of your youth
    and remember no more the reproach of your
        widowhood.
For your Maker is your husband—
    the LORD Almighty is his name—
the Holy One of Israel is your Redeemer;
    he is called the God of all the earth.
The LORD will call you back
    as if you were a wife deserted and distressed in spirit—
a wife who married young,
    only to be rejected," says your God.
"For a brief moment I abandoned you,
    but with deep compassion I will bring you back.
In a surge of anger,
    I hid my face from you for a moment,
but with everlasting kindness
    I will have compassion on you,"
says the LORD your Redeemer. (Isa. 54:4–8)

I realized I had felt humiliated. I was humiliated that I had given my heart, body, and time away to people who rejected and deceived me. I had deceived myself. I was humiliated by my own choices. I was afraid of the shame that my past carried. And here the Scriptures were saying not to be afraid, that I wouldn't be put to shame or be humiliated. Then I got to verse 9, and I felt the presence of God fall all around me. I had chills as I read. My breath stopped. I was shocked that I had just been looking up passages about Noah, because of the rainbows I had seen in my eyelashes earlier. The message I saw was that God was not angry. But here my eyes filled with tears as I read:

"To me this is like the days of Noah,
    when I swore the waters of Noah would never again
        cover the earth.

So now I have sworn not to be angry with you,
> never to rebuke you again.
Though the mountains be shaken
> and the hills be removed,
yet my unfailing love for you will not be shaken,
> nor my covenant of peace be removed,"
> says the LORD, who has compassion on you.
"Afflicted city, lashed by storms and not comforted,
> I will rebuild you with stones of turquoise,
> your foundations with lapis lazuli.
I will make your battlements of rubies,
> your gates of sparkling jewels,
> and all your walls of precious stones.
All your children will be taught by the LORD,
> and great will be their peace.
In righteousness you will be established.
Tyranny will be far from you;
> you will have nothing to fear.
Terror will be far removed;
> it will not come near you." (vv. 9–14)

The line about *tyranny* being far from me stood out. I was taught from childhood to always be on my guard against tyranny. This was a foundational stone in my orphan mindset. I learned it on my own from seeing the men around me abandon and abuse. Now, after everything I'd gone through, the only safe place I could find was in being on my own with God. But I felt like he was trying to show me that I didn't have to live in fear.

I felt like he was teaching my heart that it was good to come to him, to trust in him. But he didn't want me to do it out of fear of being hurt. He wanted me to do it out of love. Out of knowing that *he* is the place from where life flows. Out of hope and faith and freedom from fear. I prayed that I would receive all of the revelation he was giving me. I prayed that I would live life out of faith, hope, love, and freedom.

Then I climbed back down from the roof of the bus and slipped in the door. Only our tour manager, Scotty, was awake.

"You look happy this morning," he said from behind his computer.

"I feel happy," I sniffled, thankful to have cried in a way that made my heart grow on my "date" with Jesus.

Remember Josh?

It was around dinnertime.

"Lacey?" Scotty called to me from the front lounge. "Do you remember that guy from yesterday named Josh?"

My stomach flipped.

"Yes?"

"He wants to know if he can have your number."

I just stared at him. My heart was racing. I thought of the Scriptures I'd *just* read that morning. I would not walk in fear of my past hurts. I would trust God to protect me and keep me safe. I knew that if Josh were to pursue me, I would let him. But I would always be watching to look where God would take it.

"Yes," I slowly answered.

I covered my mouth in surprise at my own words.

A couple hours later, my phone chimed.

Hi, Lacey, this is Josh. Scotty gave me your number. I hope that's okay. Give me a call when you have some time. I'd love to stay in touch.

My heart dropped to the bottom of my feet. I was standing by my bunk when the text came in, so I shoved my phone underneath my pillow and walked quickly away, praying silently.

Help me not to be afraid, Lord. Help me not to lose my relationship with you. Help me to be safe. Help me. I didn't look at my phone again until after our show. Finally, I felt peace fill me as I went to respond.

> Hey, Josh, if you want to talk, the show is done and I have some time.

Two-Hour Talk and a Dove

That night we talked for two hours straight. The craziest part of the conversation was toward the end.

"Well, I guess I'll let you go. Maybe we can talk tomorrow," he said.

"Yeah, that would be cool," I answered.

"I hope you have good dreams," he said.

"Yeah, you too," I answered.

"I had a strange dream this morning, actually. It was sort of mystical."

"What happened?"

"All I remember is that I was lying in bed looking at the ceiling and a white dove appeared. I was kinda freaking out in my dream that a dove just appeared in my room, but I could feel its wings moving and pushing air onto my face. It felt magical, kinda. Then I woke up. When I opened my eyes, I was lying in my bed looking at the same spot on my ceiling where I had just seen the dove in my dream. It seemed to mean something, but I don't know what."

"That's so crazy, 'cause I was just reading about Noah this morning. For Noah, a dove was a symbol that the flood was going down and it was almost time to start a new life in a new world. It was a sign of hope for him."

183

"Wow, yeah, maybe it was just a sign of hope. I didn't think about that."

"Well, g'night."

"Bye," he answered.

After I hung up, I felt all the whimsical feelings of having met someone who was easy to connect with. Someone who listened and made me laugh and think differently about things and encouraged me in all the right ways. I felt like I had a new friend. And then I recognized all these things felt familiar. I wondered about whether it was safe. So I texted Eric Patrick.

> Hey, Eric. Call me when you have a chance. I need to talk to you and Sarah about something.

My heart was heavy as I turned off my phone and got ready for bed. I prayed for God to protect me. That night I read over that passage in Isaiah 54 again. Peace washed over me, and I fell asleep with joy.

Three days later, Eric called.

Hero Note:
Joshua Sturm

Meet Joshua Sturm. He is a hero to me because of so many things. I blush when I think of them all. But when I step back from being his wife and look at him as a child of God, bringing light into the world, I am astounded by his humility. He has a humble confidence that comes from understanding his value as a son. He has taught me so many things about how to trust God for his timing and doing things in God's gentle way. The patience he carries produces miracles of glory everywhere he goes.

Here is a note to you, from Joshua.

Dear Reader,

Don't wait to change. That still small voice you can sense is directing you toward true freedom and joy. You will realize your current "freedom" was actually slavery.

If I could give advice to my younger self, I would say discover what the word **kairos** *means. God's timing is perfect, so don't waste time worrying. Your heavenly Father knows all your hopes, fears, and dreams.*

Joshua
husband, father, musician, songwriter, graphic designer, artist

---

When the moon is shining bright, and the stars have all aligned, wait. I will be with you. When the day feels so alive, and the darkness seems contrived . . . wait. I will be with you.

Joshua Sturm, "Still Standing"

20

THE MYSTERY OF
Waking Up to Romance

I adjure you, O daughters of Jerusalem, by the gazelles
or the does of the field, that you do not stir up or
awaken love until it pleases.

Song of Songs 2:7 ESV

*W*hat's going on, Lace?" Eric asked.

"I met a guy."

"Really?"

"Yes. And he loves Jesus."

"Well, that's good. When did you meet him?"

"Tuesday. On Wednesday he called and asked for my number from Scotty. We talked for two hours that night after the show."

"That's a long time, huh?"

"Eric, I'm embarrassed to say this next part."

"What?" he said with a chuckle.

"The next day I had a day off." I paused, nervous to be honest. Blushing, I finally got it out. "Eric, we talked for six hours straight."

"Wow. Six hours straight is a long time to be on the phone, huh?"

"I swear it didn't feel that long."

"I'm sure it didn't. How about this. How about you give him my number, and let him know that you want him to call and talk with me so I can get to know him a little bit?"

I felt my heart flutter with joy at Eric's words. I felt so safe and strange that I wanted to cry. Is this what it's like to have someone watching over your heart, a father's protection?

A father protects.

Tears fell as I answered his suggestion.

"Okay. Thank you."

"I'll talk to you soon, Lace. Sarah says hi. We love you, girl. We're so proud of you."

A father provides.

"Thanks, Eric. I love you guys too. Tell Sarah I love her."

"I will."

Not long after that my phone rang again. It was Josh. I felt my heart pound as I answered and realized I was nervous to tell him about Eric. I wasn't sure how it would sound. I wasn't sure what he would think about it. I mean, we were grown people. Did we really need someone to supervise us?

"Hello?" I answered.

"Hi," came his sweet voice.

My stomach flipped with nervousness as I told him.

"I'm glad you called. I need to talk to you about something."

"What's up?"

"See, there is this guy who has been like a pastor to me over the years. I look at him like a spiritual dad, kinda."

"Yeah?" he said, sounding curious.

"Yeah. It's just that you and I have been talking a lot. And I was wanting to know if you would call and talk to him, so he can get to know you a little bit."

There was a pause of silence from us both. I felt like I should explain more.

"I have been through a lot in my life romantically, and I have asked him and his wife, Sarah, to look out for me in this area of my life. So that's why I think you should give him a call. What do you think?"

"I think that's a great idea. I think it's wise for both of us to have someone like that we can talk to. I actually have people in my life like that too."

I was amazed. I expected him to make fun of the idea. I had never heard of anything like this in my life. Except in old movies. It seemed to be something from ancient times or for arranged marriages—something they'd do in a different world. I couldn't believe Josh was agreeing to this and seemed happy about it. I couldn't believe he had a similar relationship in his own life.

"Okay, well, I guess I'll talk to you after you connect with him."

"Sounds good, Lacey. I'll talk to you soon."

Korey Says God Will Meet You Where Your Faith Is At

The next day I called my friend Korey. We'd met earlier that year when our bands toured together. She plays guitar and keyboards in the band Skillet. I told her the whole story about not wanting to get married, feeling like I should make sure I wasn't being religious about it, fasting and praying, and reading the book that suggested I make a list. Finally, I told her about Josh. How he fit so much of my list. She told me a little of her own story of meeting her husband, John, who sings and plays bass with her in Skillet.

"God will meet you where your faith is at," she said. "If you have faith for God to guide you and pick your husband like you prayed he would, and if you exercise your faith as you walk through this, then God will meet you in that journey. Everyone's story is different because everyone's faith is in a different place. But if this is what you really want, and you have the faith to wait for it to be from God and not something you manipulate and to carry on the relationship in the way God would want you to, then God will meet you there. Because that's the way he is in all things. He meets us where our faith is at."

It really blew me away to think about God being so gentle with us. Giving us what we want according to our faith. Waiting on us to be ready, never forcing us to do things in a certain way. Providing protection, blessing, discipline, and correction whenever we are willing and softhearted enough to see it. But if not, he would wait for us to want him to be involved. It's like he stands by with a heart of love and will be as involved as you want him to be.

Pacing Is Wise

Our tour was headed to El Paso, so we routed our trip through our hometown in Temple, Texas, and took a day off. We kept our band gear and our cars at James's house, and as soon as the bus pulled into the driveway, I grabbed my bag, got in my car, and drove two hours from James's house to Eric and Sarah's. I was greeted by "Welcome Home, Lacey" signs colored by their kids and big hugs from everyone. My bus call was at James's later that night for our eight-and-a-half-hour drive to El Paso the next morning.

I snuggled into the couch and fought off the urge to fall asleep. Sarah was giggly and smiley as we got into a conversation about Josh. Eric sat quietly next to her.

"Your dad talked to Josh!" she joked.

"So, what did you think?" I wondered, wide-eyed, biting my fingernails, knowing that I would take whatever he said with reverence.

"It was so cute!" Sarah giggled. "He didn't talk to him till late, so I had already gone to bed." She explained how Eric was excited to finally have permission from me to protect my heart in this way. I'd invited him to look out for me. He was so lovingly ready to kick this guy to the curb, since he expected no one to be good enough for his girl!

Sarah went on, "He walked into the bedroom after their conversation with this concerned expression. So I asked what was wrong, and he goes, 'I'm so mad.' So I became concerned! I was like, 'Why, honey?' And he says, with this deeply disappointed look on his face, 'Because I like him!'"

The two of us burst out laughing.

"You like him?" I squeaked.

Eric just kind of stared at us with a smirk, pausing before he spoke. "Well, he was just so ready to listen and just easy to talk to, and yeah, I really did like him."

That's when we went into exactly how Josh and I met and all the things we had discovered about each other since then.

"I just feel like I'm slipping into this so quickly and it makes me so nervous," I said.

"Well, think about this. What is more intimate than lying down and talking into someone's ear? And doing that for hours? It's just gonna bring you closer emotionally. The longer you do that, the closer you'll get and the more quickly it will happen. I think pacing yourself, like you want to do, is wise."

"So, how do I do that?"

"Well, maybe you should come up with some boundaries for your phone conversations."

"Like what?"

"Like maybe put a time limit on it and let it be at certain times of day."

"Like how much time? And what time of day?"

"Lace, this is something you can figure out. You just decide what you want to do."

"But Eric, I am so bad at this. I really have no idea."

"Just think about what would feel comfortable to you."

"Eric, I talked to the guy for six hours straight the other day. I have no idea about any of this. Can you please just make something up for me? I want you to just tell me. Please?" I begged.

"Are you sure you want me to come up with the time and all that?"

"Yes, I'm positive. I honestly have no idea what that would look like."

He tilted his head and looked up at the ceiling like he needed to think it through. I could tell it wasn't what he expected me to need from him and also that he didn't feel comfortable making rules for me in such a direct way. He valued my freedom so much.

A father protects.

But he also wanted to honor my request for him to help me in this way and make things safer for me.

"Well, what about twenty minutes? Twice a day? And just try not to talk when you're tired or lying down, like right when you're gonna fall asleep or just wake up. Because those moments are so personal, and it can feel really intimate to be with someone in your ear at those times. And then maybe you can have a sort of date night where you talk for a couple hours on the weekends, since your relationship is mostly over the phone while you are traveling so much."

My stomach flipped and I was so happy to hear him explain it this way. This is exactly what I wanted to understand and learn.

"I think that makes total sense. And I'm so thankful that you're willing to help me make those boundaries."

"Well, good!"

"It's almost time for me to go back to the bus. Please pray for me when I call him, because I don't want to care if he thinks I'm a total weirdo for saying we can only talk twenty minutes at a time, twice a day." I laughed, feeling so safe and loved.

"Okay, we will do that," they said. Sarah hugged me and I left the house so excited to have spiritual parents to walk with in my life.

Now, I completely understand that everyone has different circumstances and personalities and histories. Just because someone wants to date with a pure heart doesn't mean that what Josh and I went through to have that purity is the right thing for everyone. But I'm so glad that my heavenly Father met me where my faith was. He lovingly honored my desire to honor Josh's heart and my own with purity in the way that was best for us.

Josh Leading Me to Jesus and Not Himself

As Josh and I implemented boundaries on our phone calls, they actually became so much richer. They weren't deeply personal, but the time restraint created a rich tension that made them so much sweeter. I began to understand that much of the romance lay in that tension. This is what makes being a mystery so beautiful and attractive. It creates the most fantastic romantic tension.

Josh had been talking to Eric weekly as well, and began to better understand what the boundaries were actually building and protecting. I didn't realize how well he was understanding all of this until one day I was going through a minor tragedy with my family.

I ended a phone call with a relative and was sobbing when I saw Josh's name pop up on my phone. I was relieved to have a friend to talk to, and answered the phone sniffling.

"What's wrong?" he asked.

"It's my family. There are some really sad, scary things going on."

I wept for a minute before I could share a little of the story with him.

He was quiet for a long time before he finally shared with me what he had been praying during his silence.

"Lacey, I really want to be there for you while you are going through this. I care about you a lot and I want to be the one to make things feel better." He paused again before he finished. "But

I don't think it is the right time for me to be that person in your life. And I think you should go to Jesus so he can comfort you."

Even the mention of the name of Jesus was like a warm blanket wrapping around me. I knew he was right. I was so thankful for his caution and respect. He was respecting our boundaries and pace. He knew that going into a deep place emotionally would push us closer than we wanted to be at that time. And I already knew that Jesus was the right person to run to. I could have been hurt by this, but if I had it would have shown that my heart was expecting Josh to be something he wasn't meant to be at that time. I was comforted to find my heart filled with peace and love, and even joy, at the way he led me to Jesus instead of to himself.

Planting Seeds for Marriage

Something wonderful happened when Josh and I respected the pace in our dating. We became gardeners. Not in real life but in our romantic life. We cultivated ways of dealing with struggle, pain, and even victory in our relationship at this early stage. Little did we realize how those early seeds of boundaries would carry into our marriage years later.

When something came up that I needed to go to God for, instead of to Josh, it taught me how to be able to do that in our marriage later on. There are times when Josh is so wonderful and so strong, and I am lifted up by the way he treats me. But there are also times when he is struggling and needs help himself. So, because I learned this lesson in dating, it was already a habit when we went through this in our marriage. And instead of making his dark season worse by being offended that he couldn't be Jesus for me, I had learned to go to Jesus instead of Josh and let Jesus fill up my heart so that I could be the one to lift Josh up in prayer and love. And it worked the other way around as well. He learned the same lessons that carried into our marriage too. Our first love is always Jesus, whether we're single, dating, or married.

When we made boundaries in the way we talked on the phone, it planted seeds of emotional purity in our marriage as well. We could see the nuances of when the call was too long and was leading us in deeper than we wanted to be. We could sense the personal nature of hearing each other when were tired in the mornings or at night, and understood how this was more intimate than what we wanted at the time. Not only did it save those things for romantic moments as husband and wife later on, but it also made us aware of how these simple things really can be unintentionally personal but still too intimate in certain situations. We began to recognize it in our other relationships with friends and acquaintances as well.

So after we were married we understood even better how to guard our hearts in relationships with people outside our marriage. Our boundaries taught us how to avoid growing intimately connected in these ways with someone who isn't our spouse. All of this was actually teaching us how to be faithful. It was teaching us to tend to the roots of faithfulness in marriage.

How do you just turn off your flirtatious personality once you're married? I don't think you can do that. You can't just turn it off. It's a struggle to retrain your heart. But if you are in a guarded and intentional relationship with your spouse before you get married, your whole dating relationship teaches you how to not flirt with someone you desire romantically. It teaches you self-control and honor and timing.

During our dating relationship, I wanted to honor Josh's wife. I continued to pray for her, not certain if it was me or not. I was more and more certain every day that if he were to ask me to marry him one day, it would be safe to say yes. But if he never did, then I would rejoice for being given the opportunity to pray for his wife and their future. I also prayed for whoever it was that God had for me, if, indeed, he had marriage for me in the future.

Moments like these with Josh reminded me of my First Love. My First Love will always be my relationship with Christ. No matter how great of a man Josh is, he will never be Jesus. And whenever I try to put him in place of Christ, he will always do a bad job of being God for me. It's too much weight to place on someone—to expect them to be what only God can be for you. Letting God be God has provided me with so much freedom. I rejoice in it! He is so faithful and good at loving, blessing, and protecting us.

After I listened to Josh's advice, he let me go and I locked myself in the back lounge of the bus. I put on worship music and laid on my face and prayed for my family. The music spoke faith into my heart. I remembered all the peace that comes with having a heavenly Father who is sovereign and good and who cares about your loved ones more than you ever could.

A father protects.

Hero Note:
Korey Cooper

Meet Korey Cooper. She is a hero to me because she is a woman of astounding wisdom and insight. She is an artist in the way she responds to life. Her faith is at the center of everything she does. So, when she puts her hand to something, beauty erupts.

Here is a note to you, from Korey.

Dear Reader,

Life is so short. This message is all around us and yet rarely do we take the time to notice. All the success the world has to offer eludes our grasp as we breathe our last breath. I've always wanted to live for eternal things, no matter the cost. I've always wanted my life to speak of the beauty of the Lord, his love and redemption, and the fulfillment that comes from serving his purposes.

When I was young, I was zealous to serve God. I was excited that God had a destiny for my life and that he could make me a world-changer. I was driven by this passion and ready to do anything to see the advancement of the kingdom of God on this earth.

If I could go back to my younger self, I would tell myself it's not about "my" destiny, or "great things" I can accomplish for God. I would tell myself that God doesn't need me to do anything for him but that it's a blessing to simply love and know him. I would tell myself what an honor it is to serve God in the shadows where no one will ever know. I would tell myself that the greatest thing I can "do" for him is to love and serve others, and to continually speak courage into their bones.

With the Father's love,
Korey Cooper
wife, mom, musician, songwriter, superhero

21

THE MYSTERY OF
Boundaries

If your goal is purity of heart, be prepared to be thought very odd.

Elisabeth Elliot[1]

*H*i, Lacey girl!" Sarah's voice was full of joy.

I'd been trying to get ahold of her since I found out I needed to go see my voice doctor in Pittsburgh. It just so happened that Josh lived in Pittsburgh and had offered to give me a place to stay while I visited. I wanted to know the best way to handle going out to visit him. I was curious and anxious to hear what she would say.

"I have been praying for your visit with Josh. Isn't it so cool that your appointment is in Pittsburgh?"

"Is it?" I asked. "I don't know."

"Yes! Lace, you can do this well. I believe in you so much."

"So what does that look like, though? How do I stay with him out there?"

"Well obviously you aren't gonna stay with him, right?"

"Yeah, he said he would sleep at his parents' house and let me stay at his apartment. And also I could stay with Kendyll, some."

"Well, this trip should be about you getting to know him in person. Since you have mostly spoken to him only on the phone, this trip should be you just seeing how he acts around his friends and family. This is really you getting to know him better as a person, a brother, a friend, a son—that kind of thing. It's not about holding hands or being alone together, or any of that, really."

My heart sank.

What? We can't be alone together? I thought. And what does she mean we can't hold hands? I am twenty-six years old, and if he wants to hold my hand what's the big deal with that?

Now Sarah hadn't said we "couldn't" hold hands. I don't think she would have ever told me I couldn't do something. But I took her suggestions seriously because I deeply desired purity. I knew if she suggested something I'd either honor it to the extreme—or I figured I would smudge her advice in the moment until she might as well have said nothing to me at all!

I wondered at her words in silence.

I thought about the fact that I was the one who had asked her to set boundaries for me. I thought about the fact that I was grown-up and could decide for myself. But I also thought of the fact that I had done such a horrible job deciding what "safe" looked like for me in the past. This very moment was the whole reason I had asked her to walk with me.

Was she suggesting I go against Scripture? No. She was championing me to honor it. So, although I didn't understand it, and although I didn't want to, I chose to become Sarah's daughter in that moment and honor her as a mother. I sighed deeply, knowing that I would listen to her advice. If this trip was horribly boring, then at least it would still be safe.

Four-Wheeling with Parents

We finished our tour and I headed straight to Pittsburgh. I hadn't showered in several days, and I looked it. Josh picked me up at the airport. But when he saw me he greeted me with the warmest, most genuine smile. He explained that we would go straight to his parents' house from the airport because they wanted to take me somewhere special.

"But I need to shower."

"No, you don't understand, my parents aren't like that. You don't need to look any certain way."

"But I just want to shower for myself, really."

"Well, you can do that when I take you back to the apartment."

"But where are we going to go that's special? I'm definitely *not* especially presentable."

"It's okay! I promise. Trust me."

He smiled with such genuine love that I stopped arguing. The words "trust me" stuck in my head as we drove along the Pennsylvania highway listening to Metallica. I wondered about the deep meaning those words held. Then I thought, *This is exactly what I am learning. Trust.* I felt like Josh was touching the scar in my heart with his request that I trust. And every time I trusted, despite my "orphan street smarts," I felt the scar heal a little more. I would trust.

In this case, it meant believing that his parents were not going to judge my greasy hair or my shirt that was beginning to smell more and more like a dainty, feminine gorilla.

We pulled into their neighborhood, and it looked like the neighborhoods of the kids I had never felt good enough to hang out with. The house was nice and simple from the outside. When we got up to the door, I was so nervous to meet his parents I could barely talk, because I worried they would judge my homely, unwashed presence. But before we even knocked on the door, it swung open.

"Hi, Lace!" came two unfamiliar, loud, and joyful voices in unison.

Josh's dad was standing there with the biggest open-mouthed smile I had ever seen. His arms were spread wide open and before I knew what was happening he had lifted me off of my feet and was snuggling me tightly. He set me back down and stepped aside so his wife could do almost the exact same thing. She was almost squealing with joy.

"We're so glad to meet you!"

"I'm Larry!" said Josh's dad.

"And I'm Cheryl," she said, leaning in to kiss my cheek.

"Hi." I smiled nervously, stunned at such a welcome.

"Well, let's get going!" Josh's dad said excitedly. "We're taking you someplace special," he said, looking out of the side of his eye with a sneaky grin. "I'll get the jeep."

"Um, can I use the restroom first?" I asked.

"Sure!" said Cheryl as she escorted me to the bathroom.

As soon as I was alone I did what my mom always called a spit bath. I washed my armpits and reapplied my deodorant. I put on some body spray and tried to make sure my hair was as good as I could get it. I couldn't change into a clean shirt because they were all dirty from being on tour. I looked at myself and shrugged my shoulders. "Whelp, if they don't like you, then at least God does. He's the one who made you have to need showers and kept you from being able to get one," I said to the mirror. I laughed how ridiculous I felt and how out of control and how completely free I was to be myself. I was happy to be certain I wasn't manipulating this into some grand love story. And if it turned into one, it would have to be miraculous all on its own.

I turned off the light and headed outside. The jeep was parked in their yard and Josh's mom and dad were in the back. Josh was in the driver's seat and they'd left the passenger-side door open for me. I climbed in and off we went, down some side streets. Finally it looked like we were going straight down a dead-end street. But before I had the chance to be curious, we had jumped the curb and were driving into the woods. Cheryl and Larry laughed at the bewildered look I'm sure was on my face.

"You ever been four-wheeling before, Lace?" Larry asked me.

"Not in the woods," I answered nervously.

They all laughed and joked with each other while we weaved in and out of trees, went up and down hills, and finally stopped at the edge of a fast-rushing creek.

Josh jumped out of the car and came over and opened the passenger-side door. "Your turn to drive." He smiled.

"What?"

"You get to drive through the creek!" he exclaimed.

"Wait, what are you talking about?"

"All first-time guests must drive the jeep through the creek all on their own," laughed Larry from the backseat. "House rules!" he added.

"Yep! That's the rules!" Cheryl laughed.

I looked at Josh, bewildered. I had never driven a jeep before at all, let alone through a fast-moving creek I couldn't tell the depth of.

"It just doesn't seem very safe," I said to Josh, freaking out a little. "I mean, I'll have your parents' lives in my hands. I'm not very comfortable with that."

He kept smiling. "It's okay. You'll be fine. I'll talk you through it. Trust me."

There was that request again. Trust me. I don't think he understood the depth of what he was asking me to do. Again I felt the Lord speaking to me, touching the scar in my heart, asking me to go on this adventure of trust. I looked out at the rushing creek in front of me. The spray was shooting up and hitting the light, making little rainbows. I sighed and smiled through my nervousness.

"Okay," I said to Jesus, although it probably sounded like I was speaking to the Sturm family, who had ganged up on me to drive this jeep into the water. They cheered at my acceptance of the challenge.

Sitting in the driver's seat, I asked an obvious question. "So where do I go?"

"Just straight," Josh said with confidence.

"Just straight," I repeated. "Into that?"

"Yep," he answered. "Just go straight ahead."

I closed my eyes and hit the gas, and in we plunged. The water splashed all around us and the jeep thrashed around on the rocks below. Cheryl was calling out to Jesus to help us. I just kept my foot on the gas and my eyes closed and prayed with her. Finally, we got up to the other side of the wide creek. I lifted my head, opened my eyes, and pushed the brake for us to stop. Josh looked at me as I did this and he yelled out, "You didn't have to close your eyes!"

I laughed so hard at myself. I was tickled by our adventure. I was also laughing at my own foolishness, closing my eyes while driving through a river. But mostly I laughed at my complete freedom from embarrassment. There's no respectable way to hand over your desire to distrust and plow through a river in a jeep. It was hilarious, reckless freedom and joy.

Cheryl and Larry were laughing too, now. "I think I'm done driving," I said when I caught my breath. We switched spots and Josh drove a little ways until we came to a calmer spot in the creek.

Romantic Scenery

We all got out of the jeep, and Cheryl and Larry held hands and walked away. Josh took off his shoes and began to walk in the water. I took off mine and did the same. The sound of the water running over the stones was peaceful and lovely. The sun shot through the trees every now and then, and golden rays were slicing through the woods with the glory of heaven. It was the most beautiful place I had seen in a long time. We were quiet. We didn't hold hands. We weren't alone. And it was the most romantic moment.

Life on tour had been so chaotic. The quiet sounds of the still woods were the most beautiful music to my soul. On tour I never saw anything but concrete and alleyways and tour buses and hotels and backstage. Whenever I saw flowers or greenery, my heart leapt. I used to lie on tiny patches of green grass in mall parking lots on our days off and thank God for the dandelions. And now here I was, in the middle of the living, breathing Pennsylvania woods. It was like God was romancing us all on his own. The peace was so powerful it made me want to cry with thankfulness.

Romantic Tension of Reserving Romance

The whole trip was filled with activities that Josh planned where we did things with his friends and family. And everywhere we went, it was like God was romancing us. The less romantic we set out to be, the more romantic it was. The tension and safety were both blissful and powerful. I started to wonder how so many people miss out on the tension of holding back intentional romance and seeing how life romances you all on its own. Josh would sit down beside me and my whole heart would be on tiptoe. *Oh my, he is so close*, my heart would pine. *His hand is so close to mine*, my mind would race.

Noticing Him as an Artist, Appreciating Him as Person

I noticed things about him I don't think I would have noticed if we had been pursuing romance. I noticed the way he laughed with his brother and joked with his dad. I noticed the way he was gentle with his mom and how he was thoughtful with his friends.

I noticed the way he listened with grace when someone was disappointed and the way he was grateful for little things. I noticed how artistic he was with life, making art every chance he got. He drew on the walls, wrote on his shoes, painted with bleach, and made homemade cards for his friends and family. He loved the way people communicated with film and documentaries. He loved the passion in music. He was passionate about design and loved the way images and typography could communicate like music does behind lyrics. He was intentional and meaningful and thoughtful in his art. I was able to see this and appreciate it in him as a person, not as a boyfriend or future husband. I was so thankful for our boundaries and the way he was willing to walk with me through this season.

Jen Ledger

Meet Jen Ledger. She is a hero to me because of the way she says yes to God. It's apparent that her quiet humility makes her relatable, believable, and encouraging. But it's that same humility that allows her to step onto stage in front of millions and obey her heavenly Father by shining with the light of his love through music. She happens to be a rock star but only because she is an example of what it means to be a daughter.

Here is a note to you, from Jen.

Dear Reader,

If I could go back and speak to my younger self, I would say this: God is so much greater, stronger, and more real than you could ever imagine. Dare to be someone that lives freely in this truth! Trust him fiercely with all of your being. Have a faith that's so radical it screams "He can!" even when you know you can't. Following him is going to take you on an adventure beyond your wildest dreams. He will lead you, stretch you, and surprise you.

There will be hard times, but with every hurt he will heal and with every stumble he will raise you up. These will become your milestones and some of the most beautiful moments in your life. Don't waste another second of your time by being afraid. Instead, dare to believe: he is so powerful and his love for you is so strong that you can be fearless!

You are in his hands. You belong to him. That is the only thing that matters. Be the first to step out, embrace the challenges, step up to the calling. He is with you and he will help you. With him you can do anything, for nothing will be impossible with God (Luke 1:37).

With the Father's love,

Jen Ledger
drummer for Skillet, singer/songwriter

So we decided
to become gardeners—
we wanted to constantly plant seeds of honor.

22

THE MYSTERY OF
Purity

Bestow on them a crown of beauty instead of ashes,
the oil of joy instead of mourning, and a garment of
praise instead of a spirit of despair. They will be called
oaks of righteousness, a planting of the LORD for the
display of his splendor.

Isaiah 61:3

*B*oundaries work like the frame surrounding a beautiful
painting. For Josh and I, they enclosed a lovely vignette
that told the story of our growing love. They didn't infringe on
our love, they elevated it and helped tell the story. But ours is a
story still unfolding. That's what purity does; it begins your story,
unfolding it one decision at a time.

Learning from Our Decisions

Several months later, I had another doctor's appointment in
Pittsburgh. So I stayed with Josh and his family. Josh planned

a long, busy day full of fun adventures for us. It was such a fun day. But apparently he hadn't planned our sleeping situation very well. We'd driven forty-five minutes away from his parents' house to his brother's place. His brother had bought a three-story house built in the 1800s that he was renovating. Josh thought it would be better for us to stay out there for the night because it was next to my doctor's office and my appointment was early the next day.

It was already late when we got there. Josh took me on a little tour of the house. The whole place was a construction zone, really. No place to sit or stay, except for a couple beds in the middle of the mess in two different rooms. It was getting late, so I asked him about going to bed.

"So, where are we gonna sleep?"

He looked nervous.

"Well, I guess I didn't think this through very well, but there is only one bed for my brother and then this one."

"So are you saying there is only one bed for us to sleep in? And obviously there are no blankets or pillows to make a pallet."

"Yeah, well, I guess, you know, you could sleep on one end of the bed and I can sleep on the other."

I just stared in disbelief. "Are you serious?"

"Yeah, I don't really know what else to do. Is that okay?"

"Well, it's too late to call Eric and Sarah now. But you know we will have to tell them."

"Well, I mean, we're just gonna go to sleep, is all."

I didn't argue with him. I was so tired. I just lay down on the edge of the bed, disappointed, and went to sleep. He lay down on the opposite end and went to sleep. The next morning, after I'd gotten ready to go to the doctor, Josh apologized.

"'Hey, Lacey. I'm really sorry about last night. I feel like such a jerk not thinking about that being so awkward. We can talk to Eric as soon as you want to call him."

"It's okay. I mean, you were so respectful and it was a weird situation to figure out last-minute. I don't think it's that big of a deal."

Special Things Only a Wife Knows

I remember Eric's look on his face when I told him. I'd rarely seen such a protective look on a man's face over me.

A father protects.

"Well I'll just have to talk to Josh about this then, won't I?" he said with a knowing smirk.

"Listen, Lace," said Sarah as she leaned in toward me, so I would know that she wasn't mad or disappointed. "There is a special way a person's eyes look when they first open in the morning. There's the way they look just before they fall asleep. Their voice sounds a certain way when they whisper out their first words of the day while lying in their bed. These are things that are *special* for a wife to know about her husband. Things no one else really gets to know the same way she does. You just want to keep that for Josh's wife. Out of respect for the level of intimacy that comes with marriage."

This picture of honor made my heart twist and ache with longing for the beauty of it all. I didn't realize these seemingly insignificant moments could be set aside as gifts to a spouse. It just sounded so loving and beautiful. What else could I say or think? I understood what she meant and wanted with all my heart to value that. I understood better why it was more of a big deal than I had thought. It was about honor and respect. It was about being in the right time for the right things and keeping some things sacred and set apart for intimacy. It was about guarding both our hearts and respecting our future spouses, whoever they might be. Even if they were going to be each other, we should respect that in the right time.

When confronted with another opportunity to choose convenience or honor, we chose honor instead. And every time we did, we unknowingly planted seeds of honor in our marriage. If Josh had driven us back to his parents' house that night, then we would have slept for only four hours. But it would have planted a seed of choosing honor over convenience.

So we decided to become gardeners—we wanted to constantly plant seeds of honor—for our marriage, or for the other person we would each someday marry. When that seed sprouts and bears fruit in a marriage, it not only helps our relationships flourish with honor but it aids our wisdom in future situations with the opposite sex.

A Walk and a Story

After a year of knowing Josh, he visited me in Texas. I made dinner for us because he wanted to have a picnic by the lake.

After we finished our meal, he asked me to walk with him. We strolled quietly along the edge of the lake. The water sang its soft melody against the rocks.

We walked slowly, holding hands. I thought about how I had put on my list that our hands would line up so we could hold them easily as we walked together. I'm pretty short and he's pretty tall, but our hands, sure enough, lined up perfectly. I giggled as I thought about it. He took out his phone, found the song he wanted to play, and dropped it into his shirt pocket. Then he stopped and pulled me in to dance with him. He kept his eyes confidently in mine until I blushed and looked away. That's when he held me tighter and said my name.

"Lacey."

I met his eyes again, but it was difficult not to look away because his unwavering gaze was making my stomach flip and my face get hot.

"Two years ago I had a dream. In my dream, I was lying in bed about to go to sleep when a woman turned over and kissed me, said 'I love you,' turned away, and switched off the bedside light. I woke up from the dream and had this feeling like I had just dreamed about my future wife. I also had a feeling that the girl from the dream was the lead singer of Flyleaf. To be honest, I wasn't a fan of Flyleaf and wasn't even sure what you looked like. So I looked you up online and the pictures didn't seem to be much like my dream, but I still felt it was you who had kissed me. Shortly after this, I found out you were going to be playing in Pittsburgh."

He smirked at this part.

"So I got a little dressed up and went to the show with my brother and Kendyll. I waited around after the show and asked if you were going to come out at all. Someone said you'd already gone to bed. But Jason and Kendyll were talking to some of the crew, so we hung around a little longer. That's when I saw you walk across the stage." He smiled so wide. "You had on ripped jeans and dirty Converse shoes like mine." He laughed. "My heart started pounding and I thought, 'Oh God, you are really gonna make this happen.' Then you walked across the stage like you were going to come and sit by me. But you went to the other side and sat by my brother. I started to doubt myself. But then I thought, 'She's right there, just go talk to her.' So I walked over and said, 'Hey, we saw you guys when you played on Warped Tour.' You looked at me for half a second, gave me a look of disgust, and said, 'We never played Warped Tour.' Now, I meant to say that we had seen you on the Family Values Tour, but I was too flustered to correct myself."

He laughed again. I felt my cheeks get hot with embarrassment at what he said. I didn't remember any of that.

"So I just said to myself, 'Josh, you're an idiot. You just had a random dream. It doesn't mean anything at all.' And I left that night and didn't think about you for over a month. Then Kendyll came over and told me you guys were playing in Ohio and she wanted to go. She asked me to go with her and Mia, but I told her I didn't want to. Lacey, she begged me to go with her. I had no idea I would talk to you that night."

I marveled as I remembered that night we first became friends, and how I had written "Dream Giver" on his shoe.

"I had no idea we would connect like we did. But ever since then I've thought about you every day. So when I tell you that you are a dream come true, you know that I mean it."

He leaned in close, held my face with both hands, tilted up my chin, and kissed me for the first time. My eyes filled with tears.

Then he put his hand in his pocket, dropped to his knee, and held out a ring.

"Will you marry me?"

I gasped, covered my mouth, and cried. Just like you see in the movies.

Chuppahs, Johnny Cash, and a Savory Kiss

We had barbecue sandwiches from a place down the street, and my Aunt Mabel made the greens. My granny made the peach cobbler. My mom made the mashed potatoes. My gramps made the baked beans. Josh's mom made the cake.

My wedding was turning out to be a beautiful family affair.

My sisters and my aunt decorated the yard and back porch with lilac purple and soft green tulle. My sister's favorite color was green and my maid of honor's favorite color was purple, so we used those.

My granny made little crowns with purple flowers and green ribbons for my little flower girls. They each painted their own

little flower boxes and filled them with petals for the aisle. Josh had made the path himself with stones he buried, leading to the middle of the yard. He used cedar branches from our backyard to make a chuppah, which is a wedding altar that looks sort of like a gazebo.

In Jewish weddings, the chuppah symbolizes the bride moving into the house her husband has built for her. It is outside, with the canopy open to the heavens, to remind us that a man builds a covering for his wife and God provides covering for both. It also symbolizes God taking his people as a collective bride for himself, like he mentions in Isaiah 54 and 62. Jewish weddings in traditional chuppahs are held at dusk, right at sunset, like ours was, which is the beginning of a new day in Jewish culture, as it says in Genesis: "The evening and the morning were the first day." The chuppah was very meaningful to us, and Josh had a great time building it. We used the riser I toured with and put a canopy over the top of the four cedar posts where we would exchange our vows.

My friend Ryan played guitar and sang some of my favorite songs before the wedding began. When Johnny Cash's "The First Time Ever I Saw Your Face" came on the sound system, I took my gramps's arm on my left side, and my stepdad Michael's arm on the right. As they smiled with pride, I blushed at their love for me. They looked so handsome and strong. Memories flooded my heart of all they had seen me walk through. Me, so reckless; both of them so patient and gracious. We began our walk down the aisle to meet Josh.

215

We were both dressed in all white. His face was beaming with love. It felt like we had both been on a long journey and were finally seeing home. Eric gave a message about the sacredness of covenant and marriage. He explained how marriage is a gift from God to us. He had us repeat our vows, and finally said to Josh, "You may kiss your bride."

The kiss was long and savory, and made the whole audience start to yell with cheers. Then he swooped me up into his arms and carried me back down the aisle, through the house, and out the front door. We hopped in the car and drove down to the lake to the spot where he proposed to take a photo as the sun set on the water, with deep, bright orange and teal streaks from our artistic heavenly Father swirling across the sky. When we returned to the party, the family greeted us with cheers and we danced our first dance. The joy and tension was enrapturing. I'd never felt more beautiful, pure, or free. Or more treasured. The weightlessness of it all was an unexpected gift I rested in with joy while I danced in my husband's arms.

Daddy Daughter Dance

After this, I got to dance with the daddies God had sent into my life. Stephen Curtis Chapman's "Cinderella" narrated through the story of these men, who were gifts of God to my heart in different seasons of my life.

The first verse paints a whimsical picture of his daughter dancing as a toddler who has convinced him to stop working and play make-believe with her. So I danced with Michael, who had loved me so well as a little girl.

The next verse tells of his daughter in high school, and now she has convinced him to practice dancing for the prom. So I danced with my gramps, who is an amazingly patient and gentle teacher. He took such self-sacrificing care of me during my difficult teen years.

The last verse is about when his daughter is grown-up and she needs him to give her away and walk her down the aisle. So I danced with Eric, who, in a sense, had walked me down the aisle of dating and presenting me to Josh as more beautiful than before I'd met him. Because of his diligence, perseverance, and obedience to God, Eric covered me in the Father's love, with such wisdom. Sarah watched us dance and cried with joy and love for Josh and me. She and Eric had watched me make horrible choices. They'd watched me almost throw my life away. And they now watched me being released into a sacred romance. I danced and danced, but on the inside I was overwhelmed by joy—the joy of their seeing me heal and then given away in purity.

23

THE MYSTERY OF
Family

You are not to be called "Rabbi," for you have one
Teacher, and you are all brothers. And do not call anyone on earth "father," for you have one Father, and he
is in heaven.

Matthew 23:8–9

A few months after Josh and I married, Flyleaf landed another tour. I wasn't sure if I should tour or not, but Josh and Eric both felt like my time in the band wasn't over. I trusted they saw something I couldn't and decided to make a second record. I was nervous to go on tour because I'd had such a hard time on tour before. I felt like I got swept up in the machine of it all, and no one noticed I was being beaten up both emotionally and physically until I almost lost my voice completely or I had some crazy health problems. We didn't have proper boundaries set up to guard our hearts and make sure we not only performed well but that we were healthy—emotionally, spiritually, and relationally.

I desired that. I always tried to help set it up like that. But it was difficult. I often felt lonely in that effort. It was important, but only a few people on our team actively pursued it. I felt the weight of making sure we didn't drop off into hell—or send anyone else there. But because Eric had encouraged us, I trusted the decision would be blessed. So Josh and I ended up touring through our first year of marriage. We faced some difficult moments.

Questioning Eric and Sarah

During some of those rough times, I reached out to Eric for guidance, but he rarely responded. Eric was one of the most trusted voices I listened to when deciding to go on this tour. So his silence hurt me. Everything was falling apart internally with the band, and Josh and I were struggling in our marriage. But Eric wasn't around relationally or physically, as they had recently moved across the country to join a ministry in the urban core of Kansas City.

So I emailed him. It was harsh. I didn't mean for it to be, but Sarah took it that way. I just had honest questions.

I wrote that I'd never asked him to "take away my orphan identity." That was his idea. I said that if he had just come to us as a pastor and then quit answering his phone I would have understood. But he made himself out to be a dad, and then when all this hell was breaking loose, he was nowhere to be found. I told him I could just move on if a pastor were to flake out, but his being like a dad to me and then going AWOL reminded me of the men of my past who had abandoned those they should have loved. It made me question life itself. I told him that it hurt. I just wanted to know what to do and how to interpret his silence.

Sarah was crushed by my email. When we talked later, she responded harshly. Her words made me question our whole relationship.

And if I questioned everything they taught me, then I would have to question my relationship with Josh as well. It was devastating.

We Have Only One Father, We Are All Brothers

But then I spoke to Korey's pastor, a friend of ours named John Lalgee. I wrote to him, sharing my situation with Eric and Sarah. I told him how it made me question whether calling someone a spiritual parent was really a good idea, since it seems to cause so much hurt when they let us down. I asked him if it was better to just view one another as brothers and sisters. I told him my fear of writing off everything they taught me. My talk with Sarah had made it seem like our whole relationship was always fake or broken. John's words of reply were so powerful. I'm so thankful to have had his voice to speak clarity to my heart. He wrote,

> I think your conclusion regarding the fatherhood of God and the sibling nature of other relationships is sound. However, this does not mean that God does not use brothers and sisters in particular seasons to represent his Father heart. We should not be fearful or rejecting of this. In the end he is too jealous a God to let this temporary guardianship remain beyond its assigned time. Like the mother eagle spoken of in Deuteronomy 32 he stirs up the secure nest of his young to help them find new dimensions of maturity.
>
> Now that the time of the parenting aspect of Eric and Sarah's involvement in your life is over, you will find the grace that was given to them to accomplish this will diminish, but it is important that you love them all the more for having been the instruments of God and do all you can to cover any fleshiness that might manifest without allowing the same weight of influence you once did.

It was so relieving to realize that, in the face of Eric and Sarah's humanity and flesh, it would be wrong to write off everything I had learned from them. God wanted me to know that it was always he who was caring for me through the beautiful, vulnerable, loving obedience of his son and daughter, Eric and Sarah.

I wept at John Lalgee's words. I thanked God for Eric and Sarah. I prayed for God to bless them and asked God to help Josh and I let them know it was time to be released as their spiritual children. We needed this change in our relationship so that we could figure out how to make decisions out of our own ability to follow peace.

Being Released and Blessed

That Christmas we went to visit Eric and Sarah. We'd prayed about how to speak to them all night on that first night. The next morning, they sat us down in the living room and spoke first. Tears flowed freely from their eyes as they talked.

"Josh and Lacey, we just want to say that we love you so much. And we believe in you. We want our ceiling to be your floor and we want to release you as a spiritual son and daughter."

Josh squeezed my hand as we cried with them.

"You are wise and we are so proud of you both," they continued.

We told them that we felt the same way, about it being time. We told them how thankful we were to have them in our lives and for all that God had taught us through their wisdom. From then on, when we saw each other we related more as friends. As we did, our relationship looked different but still continued to grow.

It wasn't until several years later that we learned about all they had been through that year we toured, when I called and they rarely answered. At that time, their family went through a season of intense circumstantial and relational challenges, including deep poverty. Eric could find no work—no matter how many degrees he had or how many interviews he landed. When they had nothing to eat, someone would show up on the doorstep with food enough to get them through. Sarah shared the intimate story about Eric's deep depression. It was one of the darkest times in their lives.

"Eric's depression was so immense," said Sarah, "that some nights I was nervous to go in my bedroom because I wasn't sure if he'd still be breathing." They both testified to how they'd made it through this difficult period. "The presence of God was the only thing that got us through. We depended on daily meeting him to be able to survive. We had to draw near to him so he could fill us, because circumstantially we were so drained that we had nothing to live on but the daily bread of his presence. We had only him to feed us each drop of something to get us by, much less anything above that to offer anyone else."

Josh and I had no idea this was going on. But even if Eric and Sarah had just blown us off and had no legitimate reason to do so, it was clear that God had already called us to consider them guiltless. God himself had defended his son and daughter when he called them away from their ministry to us. He didn't require them to explain it all to us to make sure we weren't offended. I would go so far as to say that God did not permit them to explain it to us, because he wanted to show Josh and me that he alone was our father, and theirs as well. He cared for us and defended them.

After hearing their story, it was plain to see that they truly were guiltless. I felt like the guilty one for my painful, accusing reaction. Their faithful love humbled me—a truly beautiful display of God's love and glory.

Today, after several more cross-country moves, we are still living in the joy of this restored relationship. Eric and Sarah are close, trusted friends. They are part of Team Lacey online and are business partners in music and our new clothing line, Tattoo Alternative. They love our boys, who lovingly refer to them as Momma Sarah and Papa Eric. Not all pastoral or spiritual family relationships will be restored and move forward in such a connected way, but it is the heart of God for us to live reconciled and in unity.

The most beautiful thing in all the world is the freedom God gives us. We are a free family. We don't have to feel enslaved to any religious family obligations. We get to enjoy a free and genuine relationship with our loved ones, because our covenant we make to be family is a free choice and it's not slavery. It's not guilt-tripping manipulation. Because of this our love continues to be proven genuine. In the moments when God has made it clear that we are not to be the savior for one another, for whatever reason, the response from our family is to love, honor, and release each other anyway. God teaches us to love his way. And his love is pure, genuine, and free. His love is True Love in a world of broken lovers.

God created this life all around you to romance your soul,
so you would long for the author of its beauty.

Conclusion

The Son of God became a man to enable men to become sons of God.

C. S. Lewis[1]

So, there are two morals to this story I have recounted to you with both pain and joy.

The first is this: *God will be a better Father to you than any earthly father could ever be.* Although God will model his father-heart to you in different ways, his greatest joy is to have you for his own child.

How Our Heavenly Father Loves Us

JW's voice is fatherly but still professional. He has a hint of artist in his eyes but just enough levelheadedness to be a good businessman. That's why my husband and I are happy to have him managing our music career. We call him Dubbs. He always greets Josh and me with a genuine smile.

One day I noticed that the faint lines around his eyes spread farther than any smile I'd ever seen from him could reach. They seemed to have been etched into his skin by a deeper joy, some part of Dubbs we didn't know.

But I remember the day I saw it.

JW has a daughter, Jordan. Her dark chocolate–colored hair moved in waves around her shoulders and flowed down her back like a princess while she told her daddy a story I couldn't hear. She had grown into all the glory of being a young woman but still had the giddiness of a ten-year-old as she talked excitedly with her hands.

Her daddy listened intently, watching and admiring her. Even though the room was bustling with people coming in and out, it was clear that to JW there was no one else in the room.

All of a sudden, she made a comment of brilliance. Her eyes were wide as she lifted her eyebrows and tilted her head with the cleverest look on her face.

And that's when I saw it.

His daddy-smile grew so wide that he had to open his mouth, throw his head back, and laugh. He pulled her into his arms, wrapping her up in his embrace, and she buried her head against his chest. This daddy-smile over his daughter was the one I had never seen before.

This was the author of the lines around his eyes, so wide no other smile could reach them. Through his daddy-smile, he said more things that I couldn't hear, continuing to hold her in his arms for a long time. He was present, relishing the joy of their love. The moment felt both frozen and alive—somehow eternal. She eventually pulled back to go on with her story. I watched, marveling at what it must be like to pour an open-hearted conversation into your daddy's attention, knowing you are one of the highest delights in his life.

A few minutes into the next part of the conversation, Jordan started playing with her hands and fingernails. She was still talking but was looking down the whole time. Finally, she looked up and said something that seemed to be some heavy weight she was painfully pulling off of her heart. Then she looked down again and dropped her shoulders, slumping her posture into a listless-looking sadness.

She covered her face with her hands. Her shoulders bobbed as she started to weep. Dubbs pulled her into his arms again, and she laid her head on his chest and cried. He pushed her hair back from her face and let her release something that needed to be released.

Then, after a minute, she sat back up. Keeping her head down, she said something else. Her daddy gently tilted up her chin so she could see the compassion and love in his face. His eyes were wide and searching hers. He spoke to her this way for a moment before she threw herself back into his arms. He held her like a little child. The daddy-smile returned as he delighted in his princess throwing all her weight safely into his arms.

I finally stood up from where I had been strumming my guitar, marveling at the scene, and went to the porch to write a song and sort out my thoughts. The song is called "Mystery."

> I've been trying to get away from myself
> and when I try to speak up, there's no help
> but you caught me with steady eyes
> speaking low like a sunrise
> You notice me like no one else
> And it's a mystery right in front of me
> How a father loves a daughter, what does all that mean?
> And how do you know me so well
> Like you seem too . . .
> And do you really love me . . . like your eyes say you do?
> I made a plan to run away from this war
> Cause I don't want to hurt you anymore
> But you fought through my firewalls
> Above the roar I heard you call,

you rescue me like I'm yours.
I learn what love means by how you love me,
But when you love me its still hard to believe
Cause I don't understand what true love means
But I just want to thank you for waiting on me
Cause I learn what love means by how you love me,
But when you love me its still hard to receive
Cause I don't understand what purity means
But I just want to thank you for being patient with me
Cause it's a mystery, right in front of me
How a father loves a daughter
What does all that mean
And how do you know me so well
Like you seem to?
And do you really love me, like your eyes say you do . . . ?
You do.

God Loves Me Because of Christ

When I began writing this book, my father-in-law gave me a journal as a gift. Since I knew I would be exploring the topic of fathers, I decided to pursue an intentional relationship with my father-in-law to understand more about what having an earthly dad is like. We wrote back and forth for over a year.

One of the things I learned through our correspondence is *why* he loves me. He wrote:

I first began to love you because Josh loved you. I can't help feeling that way. If you are special to him, you are special to me. When your son picks someone to be with for the rest of his life, all his hopes and dreams are with her. Your love for him should pour into her. You want to know all about her. If her past was difficult, you want to comfort her. To tell her that it's in the past, and from now on she will be loved the way she should have been. You actually love her more because her heart being entrusted to you after her pain is so precious. Whatever happens to her now happens to your son. She's family forever. Truly family.

When I read this it spoke to me about how my heavenly Father loves me *because* of Christ.

The second moral to the story is this: *Christ is our true love in this world of broken lovers.*

Imagine life as a beautiful painting. A masterpiece from God. Then we make a choice with our freedom to reject God and his plans and go our own way. Our sin is like throwing a random splotch of paint over a detailed, intricate, and purposeful landscape.

And afterward the enemy of our souls will say one of two things. He'll say, *Your splotch is beautiful and it looks better this way; keep throwing paint,* and in the end it is a mess with no purpose and chaos and confusion and no peace at all. Or he might say to us, *Oh, look at how you ruined everything. You'll never be able to fix it. It's so ugly! You should give up because God will never love you; look at what you did to his masterpiece. Don't even think of asking forgiveness; you don't deserve it!*

Both of these are lies. These lies are meant to "limit" our infinite and gracious God who created the whole universe and everything in it. But his love is *limitless.*

Here is what God says when we throw splotches of sin onto the masterpiece filled with glorious plans for us: *Are you going to turn to me now? Because if you do, I can make this so beautiful.* And with each new splotch it's the same question. He stands with a paintbrush covered in the blood of Christ, watching our every move, waiting for the moment when we will turn to him. *How about now, my love? Will you turn now? Because this is going to be amazing if you do.*

And when we throw more splotches, he says again, *Oh, I can see this moment so beautifully turning into mountains of strength*

and flowing rivers of understanding and compassion through you
if you will turn now. Will you turn now?

So long as there is breath in our lungs, we will always have the Lord standing over our lives with his paintbrush, waiting on us to turn to him and allow him to make a new masterpiece out of our messes. I almost missed out on all the beauty he intended to paint with my mess because I couldn't believe that he could do anything with me, a divorced adulteress who was unfaithful to him.

But when I was deceived and still living in my orphan mindset, the Lord pursued me like a loving father or a jealous husband. He surrounded me with people who prayed for me and loved me in the midst of my deception by telling me truths I didn't want to hear. And when I'd rejected that truth, he handed my soul over to the evil I was chasing. I was tangled in a web of deception.

As the web tightened around me and began to choke the life out of me, I remembered the only One who ever gave me life was Christ. So when I cried out to him in truth and sincerity, he rescued me again, like a loving father or a faithful husband, full of forgiveness and reconciliation before a lost daughter or an adulterous bride.

Christ's heavenly love is always available to everyone, regardless of whether we have a loving earthly father or earthly romance in our lives or not. We are at all times invited by Christ to pursue and enjoy a "true love" relationship with him both now and forever. It is the only true and perfect love we will find on earth. He considered a relationship with you worth dying for. I have found that my relationship with Christ has been more than worth everything it has cost me. He is forever worthy.

Jesus, the Christ

Meet Jesus. He is a hero to me because without him nothing would exist. Without his love and grace I would not know what *true* love is. He is everything I have ever longed for. He is sufficient for all my needs and my heart's desire. I will never be able to out-give him, or out-dream his dreams for me. He is the greatest adventure this life has to offer. And he is life eternal.

Here is a note to you, from Jesus.

Dear Beloved,

God has made you so beautiful and unique.[1] His fingerprints are all over you. He knows why you cry and what makes you laugh.[2] He loves it when you light up with joy and are moved with awe.[3] He created this life all around you to romance your soul, so you would long for the author of its beauty.[4] He has seen every hurt you have endured. He has bottled your tears.[5] He has always loved you.[6] Even before you abused the freedom he gave you by misusing his gifts, he already made a way to forgive you and restore you.[7] When you chose death in your sin,[8] he chose to send me,[9] the Word of God made flesh,[10] the Son of God,[11] to teach you how to live as a child of God.[12] Then he chose me to die in your place so you never have to die for your sins.[13] I rose from the dead and defeated sin, death, and hell forever. Now, when your body wears out, your soul and spirit will live forever, if you put your faith in me.[14] If you follow me you will have life to the full and life everlasting.[15] You will know what it is to be loved and to love others.[16] Please don't settle for counterfeit versions of love.[17] God created you to burn with his love blazing in your heart.[18] All other loves will leave you restless and unsatisfied. You will not find the love you're searching for in any earthly father or in any earthly romance.[19] But when you find true love in God the Father and in me through the Holy Spirit, then you will be free to give and receive true love from heaven here on the earth.[20] And when you experience and display love on earth as it is in heaven, then you will burn with the blazing fire of purity and purpose you were created for.[21] I am True Love in this world of broken lovers.[22] And so are you . . . when in lovesick obedience,[23] with grace to overcome,[24] you are transformed[25] into who you were always meant to be, a child of God,[26] the bride of Christ,[27] the temple of the Holy Spirit.[28]

Love,

Jesus

(1) Ps. 139:14; (2) Job 8:24; (3) Isa. 63:1; (4) Job 37:14–16; Ps. 19:1; 33:5; Rom. 1:20; (5) Ps. 56:8; (6) Jer. 31:3; (7) 1 Pet. 1:20; Rom. 8:29; Rev. 13:8; (8) Deut. 30:15; (9) John 3:16; (10) John 1:1; (11) 1 John 4:15; (12) 1John 3:10; (13) Rom. 4:25; (14) 1 Cor. 15:54–57; (15) John 10:10; Matt. 16:24–26; (16) John 13:34; 15:13; (17) 1 John 4:8; 1 Cor. 13:1–13; (18) Matt. 3:11; Heb. 12:29; (19) Ps. 16:2; 2 Cor. 5:7; (20) John 13:35; Phil. 1:9–11; (21) Eph. 2:10; (22) 1 John 3:16–18; 4:8; 1 Cor. 13:1–13; John 15:3; 3:16; Rom 13:10; 1 Pet. 4:8; (23) John 14:23; (24) Rom. 6:14; (25) Rom. 12:2; (26) Gal. 3:26 (27) Isa. 54:5; Rev. 21:9–11; Eph. 5:27; (28) 1 Cor. 6:19.

Afterword

by Greg Laurie

What about you? Have you "found true love in a world of broken lovers"?

Maybe you've been scarred and mistreated by people in life. Maybe you've experienced abuse, neglect, hostility, or indifference in your relationships. Maybe, like Lacey, you have been living your life with an "orphan identity." Maybe you, too, are skeptical when you are told that a father's job is to protect, provide, and correct.

Then again, maybe you've experienced solid, healthy relationships in your life. Maybe you've had excellent examples of fathers, husbands, and leaders. Maybe you've experienced deep love in your life, but there's still a void that hasn't been filled—a deeper love you are still yearning for.

Whatever the case, know this: God designed you to know True Love, and it is found only in his Son. You can know and experience True Love through a relationship with Jesus Christ. Here's how:

1. Admit that you are a sinner.

That is hard for some people, but it's absolutely essential. Before you can be found, you have to admit to being lost.

In Romans 3:23, the Bible says, "All have sinned and fall short of the glory of God." Every one of us has broken God's commandments. Every one of us has fallen short of God's standards. Certainly, there are good people out there, but being a good person doesn't get you to heaven. Heaven is not for good people; it is for forgiven people. Even if you are a good person, relatively speaking, you aren't good enough.

You are not perfect, and Jesus said, "Be perfect, therefore, as your heavenly Father is perfect" (Matt. 5:48). But of course, on our own none of us are perfect, and none of us can become perfect. You fall short. You are a sinner. Recognize that and admit it to God.

2. Realize that Jesus Christ, the Son of God, died on the cross for your sin.

Yes, he died for the world, but he also died for *you*. I love the way the apostle Paul personalizes it. He speaks of "the Son of God, who loved me and gave himself for me" (Gal. 2:20).

Christ died for you. Truly. It wasn't nails that held Jesus to that cross more than two thousand years ago. It was love for you. As John 3:16 tells us, "God so loved the world that he gave his one and only Son, that whoever believes in him shall not perish but have eternal life."

Let it sink in. Let it take root in your heart. Jesus Christ died for you.

3. Repent of your sin.

What does *repent* mean? It means realizing that you have done wrong things, that you keep doing wrong things, and that you are going to turn from those things and turn to Christ instead. The Bible says, "Repent, then, and turn to God, so that your sins may be wiped out, that times of refreshing may come from the Lord" (Acts 3:19).

4. Receive Jesus Christ into your life.

Being a Christian isn't merely believing a creed. It isn't merely going to a church. Being a Christian is having Jesus Christ live inside of you as Savior, as God, as Friend. Have you asked him in yet? You will know he is there. Jesus says, "Here I am! I stand at the door and knock. If anyone hears my voice and opens the door, I will come in" (Rev. 3:20).

Only you can do that. Only you can open the door of your life. No one else can open that door for you. The doorknob of your heart, so to speak, is on the inside. The Bible says, "To all who did receive him, to those who believed in his name, he gave the right to become children of God" (John 1:12). As a son or daughter of God, you can experience the love of a heavenly Father by receiving Jesus into your life.

If you have never done that, I ask you to do it right now. I'm asking you to receive Christ, have your life changed, and have your eternal address altered from hell to heaven.

5. Do it publicly.

If you have received Jesus into your life, make a public stand for him. Jesus bled and died for you publicly, and you need to own him in your life without shame. Jesus said, "I tell you, whoever publicly acknowledges me before others, the Son of Man will also acknowledge before the angels of God". (Luke 12:8).

Communicate to others that you have made Jesus Christ the Savior and Lord of your life. If you have the chance to do that in your church, take that opportunity. If you have a chance to tell your neighbors, your roommates, your family, or people at your work that you have received Jesus, then take those opportunities. Doing so will not only please the Lord but will cement the decision in your own heart and life.

6. Do it now.

If God has been speaking to your heart, you need to do this now—not tomorrow, not in a week, but now. This could be your last opportunity to get right with God, because none of us knows when our lives will end.

You will never regret making this decision to follow Jesus. Not now. Not through all eternity.

Do you want to go to heaven when you die? Are you trying to fill a void in your life with the things this world has to offer?

You were created to know God. And you can begin a relationship with him right now. God is only a prayer away.

If you want Christ to come into your life right now to forgive your sin . . . if you want your guilt removed and want to have a fresh start in life . . . if you want to go to heaven when you die, you might pray a prayer like this one:

> *Lord Jesus, I know that I am a sinner. But I thank you for dying on the cross for my sins and rising again from the dead. I turn from that sin now and ask you to come into my life as Savior and Lord, as God and Friend. I choose to follow you from this day forward, through all the days of my life. Thank you for calling me and accepting me and forgiving me. I pray these things in your name. Amen.*

Yes, it's a very simple prayer. But if you meant it, Jesus Christ has just come into your life. Welcome to the greatest life of all—a life of True Love.

Greg Laurie

Notes

Part 1 A World of Broken Lovers

1. C. S. Lewis, *The Four Loves* (New York: Harcourt, Brace, 1960), 6, 119.

Chapter 1 The Mystery of Being Royal

1. C. S. Lewis, *Mere Christianity* (New York: HarperOne, 2001), 206.

Chapter 2 The Mystery of Needing to Be Needed

1. Jeremiah 17:5.

Chapter 3 The Mystery of an Orphan Identity

1. John 14:18.

Chapter 4 The Mystery of Fatherlessness

1. "The Extent of Fatherlessness," *National Center for Fathering*, accessed April 18, 2016, http://www.fathers.com/statistics-and-research/the-extent-of-fatherlessness/.

Chapter 6 The Mystery of Our Deathly Freedom

1. Galatians 5:13 NLT.

Chapter 7 The Mystery of Being Deceived

1. Søren Kierkegaard et al., *Works of Love* (New York: HarperPerennial, 2009), 23.

Chapter 8 The Mystery of What Love Isn't

1. Fyodor Dostoyevsky, *The Brothers Karamazov: A Novel in Four Parts and an Epilogue*, trans. David McDuff (New York: Penguin, 2003), 48.

Chapter 9 The Mystery of Freedom and Suicide

1. Søren Kierkegaard, *The Sickness Unto Death: A Christian Psychological Exposition for Upbuilding and Awakening*, trans. Howard V. Hong and Edna H. Hong (Princeton, NJ: Princeton University Press, 1983), 32–33.

Chapter 10 The Mystery of Rage and Questions

1. Andrea Danko, "Change." Used by permission.

Part 2 Finding True Love

1. Amanda Cook, "Pieces," *Brave New World*, © 2015 Bethel Music. Used by permission.

Chapter 12 The Mystery of Silence

1. Justin Taylor, "Charles Templeton: Missing Jesus," *The Gospel Coalition*, May 9, 2013, https://blogs.thegospelcoalition.org/justintaylor/2013/05/09/charles-templeton-missing-jesus/.
2. Jeremiah 29:13.

Chapter 13 The Mystery of Renewal

1. Lewis, *Four Loves*, 121.

Chapter 14 The Mystery of Choosing to Be a Daughter

1. Sarah Patrick, "The Joy of the Lord Is My Strength," *Sarah K Patrick*, May 1, 2013, http://www.sarahkpatrick.com/the-joy-of-the-lord-is-my-strength/.

Chapter 16 The Mystery of Loving an Idea versus Loving a Person

1. Ephesians 4:15 BLB.
2. John 14:15 NET, emphasis added.

Chapter 17 The Mystery of Marrying Jesus

1. Nick Hall, "Couch Sessions with Nick Hall—Identity (Part 1)," YouTube video, 3:18, uploaded by Ransom TeeVee Jan 30, 2014, https://www.youtube.com/watch?v=UpPjL0Xt77o.

Chapter 21 The Mystery of Boundaries

1. Elisabeth Elliot, *Passion and Purity: Learning to Bring Your Love Life Under Christ's Control*, 2nd ed. (Grand Rapids: Revell, 2013), 130.

Conclusion

1. Lewis, *Mere Christianity*, 179.